"Milestones to the Miraculous is a book filled wi
guide to walk in the Spirit and how to exper.
here on earth. I love the way Dr. Burpee poi   ... the word of God in
order to learn from "The Master" himself to do what He did; how Christ himself,
through the Holy Spirit, empowers us to move in miracles, signs, and wonders.
This book is a life changing journey."

- Jose Vicente Bonilla, Ph.D., MSc, BSc.

"This book, *Milestones to the Miraculous*, is an ultimate compilation of the teachings of
Pastor John Burpee. He has been teaching and mentoring us personally since 2019.
Pastor John is like the catalyst that speeds up a chemical reaction increasing
productivity rate. His mentorship helped us see our destiny and purpose with
clarity. His teachings and guidance are catapulting us towards our destiny of bearing
fruit for the Lord Jesus Christ. We highly recommend you read this book, especially
if you are waiting for a breakthrough in your ministry."

- Prabhu Deepak Udayakumar, MD & Adlene Jenita Udayakumar, MD

"I have personally known Dr. John Burpee for 8 years. He serves as my spiritual
father, functions from a place of love, and has tremendous spiritual understanding
and authority. John is a master teacher and storyteller. *Milestones to the Miraculous* is a
practical, enjoyable, step-by-step guide detailing John's experiences, encounters, and
milestones that set the course for his journey to minister in signs, wonders, and
miracles.

This book helps you better understand your identity and destiny (God-given
purpose), hear God's voice more clearly, flow with the Spirit, and come into
alignment with God's Word and His ways. John's teaching will help set you free of
a religious mindset, conquer the spirit of fear, and prepare you to receive all the
Kingdom of God offers. I highly recommend the book and John's teaching."

- Joseph, Peck, M.D. Time Doctor and The Journal Guy Founder and
  President, Empower 2000, Inc.

Milestones to the Miraculous

Receiving the Miraculous
Ministering in the Miraculous

Dr. John Guy Lockwood Burpee
Foreword by Glenn Bleakney

DEDICATION

I dedicate this book to my best friend and awesome helpmate. The main reason I am dedicating this book to her is because she has lived every aspect of this journey with me.

Nancy has been with me in my darkest hours physically and spiritually ministering to me using the principles in this book. We have traveled around the world several times doing healing crusades, minister's conferences, planting churches and Nancy has always been right by my side.

We pastored together for 25 years in four different churches and now we serve as leaders of a minister's network. Just about every milestone I went through, Nancy experienced it with me, and we grew together. At this time in our lives we are probably having the most fun we have ever had. We love traveling and ministering and we get to do it together. I love this girl!

Table of Contents

FOREWORD

I have known Dr. John Burpee for over 12 years. As a result of spending hundreds of hours together, especially during the past few years, our relationship has moved from that of collegial to close friends. John Burpee is an extraordinary leader who is a mentor and friend to many. Whether in the Church or in the marketplace, he has demonstrated an unusual commitment to help others scale barriers of resistance to move into their God-ordained purpose in the Kingdom.

One of John's favorite words is "intentional." There is nothing haphazard about fulfilling our destiny in Christ. In *Milestones to the Miraculous*, John Burpee weaves together, from Scripture and personal life lessons, a powerful treatise showing that process is just as much a part of God's plan as promise. The journey must be navigated well to enter and experience the full life God has planned for us.

I have been looking forward to the release of *Milestones to the Miraculous* by my mentor and friend Dr. John Burpee. It is highly practical and full of wisdom. Like me, I believe once you pick up this book, you will find it hard to put down. You may also find yourself going back to it again and again, gleaning critical Kingdom life lessons.

Glenn Bleakney
Awake Nations Ministries
Awakenations.org

ENDORSEMENTS

The apostle Paul said in 1 Corinthians 2:4-6 (NASB), "…and my message and my preaching were not in persuasive words of wisdom, but in demonstration of the Spirit and of power, so that your faith would not rest on the wisdom of men, but on the power of God."

Sadly, most churches and their leaders have not taken Paul's example to heart and have done just the opposite, expecting human wisdom to heal the wounds and fill the voids in men's souls that only the supernatural power of God can accomplish. Attempting to solve supernatural problems by natural means can only produce discouragement, disillusionment, and failure in the body of Christ.

Fortunately, God has raised up men like my friend, John Burpee, whose book *Milestones to the Miraculous*, is a wonderful mixture of sound biblical Christian principles and profound personal experience in the power of the Holy Spirit.

This book will provide its readers with guidelines to enter an effective partnership with God to heal the sick and release prisoners from darkness while overcoming the spirit of fear and expanding the influence of God's kingdom.

-   Joan Hunter, Author/Evangelist

I have known Dr. John Burpee for almost 30 years now. I have participated in ministry with him in church services, prayer meetings, revivals, ministry to individuals, and other arenas. I know his heart, I know his passion for Jesus, I know his family. I say these things to confirm his integrity and faith in God's power.

I am a physician by profession; however, ministry is the biggest passion I have—ministry to patients, friends, and family. Sometimes that ministry is using my God-given knowledge in the physical realm, sometimes that ministry is using my God-given knowledge in the spiritual realm. Reading *Milestones to the Miraculous* was like reading a history lesson of another doctor's life—my own. John hit so close to how God has revealed things to me in the past that I knew his revelations in this book were from the Holy Spirit and taken from his lifetime of experience. John's knowledge of God's desire for all of us to minister with the gifts that we have been given is genuine and powerful.

I frequently tell patients that they are Spirit-Soul-Body, and I can minister to all three, but my recommendation is that they get with their pastor for their spiritual ministry and I will focus on the other two (not hesitating to ask other Christian physicians to help if needed). This book's explanation of this reality will help anyone who reads it.

As you read John's writings, allow the Holy Spirit to minister to those areas in your life. This book has come into your hands for just this time! This is the opportune season for God to transform you and heal those areas that need to be healed. God has worked through John Burpee in the physical realm to bring healing, release from captivity, and now, He will work through the experiences in John's life to help transform your life.

I cannot endorse this book any higher than to say that I believe the words are empowered by the Holy Spirit to bring life-change to whoever reads it. Read it once, twice, three times or even 50 times if that is needed to release areas in your life from captivity and bring healing in your own spirit, soul, and body!

- Dr. Steve Buckles, St. Joseph, MO

This is a great book; the milestones of Dr. Burpee's life guide us to check our life's milestones and how they build our personal relationship with God. This book helps us to understand our authority and purpose for the kingdom of God. I recommend this book for everyone to read, to be blessed, and to serve the kingdom of God.

- Sheeba John, Nurse Practitioner

This book holds biblical treasures, truths, and instructions that encourage us to keep searching for the next milestone that every Christian can achieve to experience all that God has in store for his children. Dr. John Burpee laid out detailed steps that every believer can strive for in order to attain a Godly kingdom mindset which will result in a powerful spirit filled life.

- Sunil Patel, Aeronautical Engineer

There seems to be a conspiracy across much of the body of Christ with regards to downplaying the essential complementing witness of the ministry of the miraculous alongside the declaration of the Word of God.

This is in no way a new development as we see this same spirit in operation in the chief priests and scribes in Jesus's day. The limitation of overt cessationism by some seems almost equally matched by the covert cessationism that is practiced by some that would claim themselves as charismatics in the body of Christ.

John Burpee does a great service to the body of Christ in writing *Milestones to the Miraculous* as he lays a great foundation for the saints to engage with in their journey towards contending for the miraculous to be outworked in their kingdom assignments. The equipping of the saints must include this vital dynamic of the working of miracles in our midst.

I believe the timing of this book is prophetic in the sense that we are about to see a mighty release and commissioning of the 97% of the saints that are called to minister in the marketplace spheres in their cities.

John Burpee addresses the key issues that hinder many believers from operating with confidence and correct context in the ministry of the miraculous. I pray that as you read this book God will fan the flame of the work of the miraculous to go to a whole other level in your life!

- David Balestri, Prophetic Executive Consultant, National Convenor: Australian Coalition of Apostolic leaders

It has been my honor and privilege to know John and Nancy Burpee for many years. We first met in an apostolic gathering with Dr. Peter Wagner in Dallas, Texas back about 18 years ago. For as long as I have known John, he has been diligently pursuing God and experiencing the manifestations of the presence of God. It seems like everywhere that John and Nancy go there are miracles, signs, and wonders that occur. The other indicator of their ministry gifting is that many souls are added to the Kingdom of God in their meetings and in their everyday lives. They are bridgebuilders! Fathers in the Faith! Pioneers! History Makers! Miracle Workers! Servants! And most importantly Sons of the Most High!

- Marcus J. Triplett, Apostle, President of "Global Apostolic Network" and the "Supernatural Training Center" of Daytona Beach, Florida, and serves as the Secretary/Treasurer: Section V of the Peninsular Florida A/G

As my friend and apostolic covering, John Burpee has mentored me in my pursuit for more in God's kingdom. John's passion to inspire, equip, and impart has energized many throughout the world for more understanding of the kingdom of God. *Milestones to the Miraculous* contains truths and revelation for that pursuit and is a must read to receive and minister a kingdom of power, healing, signs, and wonders.

- Lois Flewelling, Author/Speaker, Hidden Treasures Within and Step into New Beginnings, President, Empowering Life Center and The Gathering

You know someone that needs miraculous healing now, or you will. It will either be you, a loved one, or a stranger in need of healing. We need to be equipped to face the challenges of sickness and the diseases that confront us daily. The instruction and testimonies written here are simple, straightforward, and full of genuine applications. Each of us needs to be equipped with the reality of God's healing truth and the power necessary to demonstrate it to the world around us— His truth is relevant today! I have known John and Nancy Burpee for over 20 years. Their words, lives, and ministry are true before the Lord and people, both believers and former skeptics. It is easy to endorse this book; it is a manual of truth and living examples that should be used regularly, not merely read and set aside.

- Bill Byers, Living Water Ministries, Intl.

This book is a MUST READ for EVERYONE who is HUNGRY to move into God's miraculous in their life. Our friend Dr. John Burpee packs this book full of personal life experiences, solid biblical principles, and amazing spiritual insights. *Milestones to the Miraculous* will help you develop a Kingdom Mindset that accelerates you on your own journey into the exciting Glory realm of God's Miracles!

- Patrick & Laurencia Huck, Co-Founders, TransformLeaders.com & TransformHumanity.org

In *Milestones to the Miraculous*, Pastor John shares his faith journey, the power of the Gospel, and how God met him in the most miraculous ways! I love how he uses Biblical principles and life lessons to teach us how we also can set up milestones and record the miracles that God has done for us in our life. But that is not all!

Pastor John helps the reader either discover or affirm their identity in Christ and guides them in overcoming the enemy and finding freedom in Jesus. These milestones are what make up an individual believer's journey of abiding, trusting, obeying, and believing in a powerful God. You will find yourself wanting more understanding of living a Kingdom minded life that is filled with the miraculous!

Pastor John and his wife Nancy are very dear to me and have added value and encouragement to my walk with the Lord. You will find yourself blessed and encouraged within each turn of the page.

- Debbie Mascioli: Biblical Empowerment Leadership Coach | Author | Speaker | Trainer | Christian Conciliator | Mediator | Growth Specialist.

Excellent! God spoke to me! Apostle Burpee has delivered a road map to freedom, anointing, and authority in the Kingdom of God. His gift as a teacher allows him to break down complex concepts into easy to grasp principles. It is both practical and prophetic as each page drips with solid teaching and revelation born out of decades of pursuing God to work miraculously on behalf of his flock and the lost.

I am reminded of Psalm 103 which says, "He made known His ways to Moses, His acts to the sons of Israel." If you want to see, experience, and be used in God's miraculous 'acts', take the time to digest this book to understand God's ways.

- Rev. Gregory S. Lloyd, Embassy of Hope Church, Huntingdon PA

This book addresses one of the most crucial areas of effective Christian living and is a MUST read … powerful, penetrating insights that are practical and highly relevant for today. Dr. John Burpee writes in a very easy to read style punctuated by honest testimony of his own journey. It is not only wonderfully empowering, but written by a man of real integrity and proven credibility. Dr. John has done us all a great service in presenting these vital truths.

- Pastor Kevin Forlong, Brisbane, Australia
  KEVIN FORLONG MINISTRIES INC, kevinforlong.org

INTRODUCTION

There are so many people that need a miracle, a healing or even a breakthrough. I believe as you read each chapter of this book you will discover Biblical principles with simple applications that will help you receive all that God intends for you.

This book is about discovering your identity, your God given purpose. It is about coming into alignment with God's Word and His ways. It is about receiving and releasing. As you go through each chapter you will find yourself getting set free of a religious mindset and coming into all of what the Kingdom of God offers. You will also learn to operate from your spirit and how to hear God's voice.

As you come to the end of this book you will know how to engage, receive, and release the Kingdom of God. Releasing salvation, miracles, signs, wonders, deliverance, and empowerment on earth as it is in heaven.

This book will inspire you to go into all the world, take territory, advancing the Kingdom of God.

Enjoy the ride!

Chapter 1
Milestone

Several years ago, I was preaching in a church in Huntingdon, Pennsylvania. During the altar ministry that Sunday morning there were many instant healings. The service was a profound meeting where the manifest presence of God was evident.

The pastor asked me at the end of the meeting, "What milestones have you gone through to get to where you are today?" I thought to myself, "That is a good question," and I have pondered it many times over the years. I concluded that this is an important question that needs to be addressed properly.

I started thinking about my journey in life, the experiences and encounters I had along the way.

I thought about the effect these experiences and encounters had on my life. How they established my heart, my faith, my foundation, and my mindset in Kingdom thinking and ministry. They were literally milestones in my life.

Years ago, in Lincoln, Nebraska while pastoring Gates of Praise, we purchased some property on 70th & Vine with a beautiful building on it. One of the places in that building that was important to me was the boardroom because this is where leadership met and made important decisions.

In my home, my car, my office, the sanctuary and even the boardroom atmosphere was critical. I knew I had a big part in creating it.

Lezlie, one of the staff pastors and I went to several stores to look for some pictures to hang in the board room and I said, "I am not looking for religious pictures, I want pictures of doors, stairs, bridges and roads. Those pictures represented areas of my life where something big happened, where faith increased, and breakthrough happened.

Those pictures represented milestones that changed my life, the bridges I crossed, doors I went through, stairs I climbed and roads I went down.

Atmosphere is so important in our walk with Jesus and these pictures reminded me and others of how we got to where we are today.

Definition

Whenever I work on an article or a message, I research the definition of the word or topic that I am addressing for better understanding and application.

So, I did a Google search of the word milestone and how it applied to my journey.

Google search: Milestone – A milestone is one of a series of numbered markers placed along a road or boundary at intervals of one mile or occasionally, parts of a mile. They are typically located at the side of the road or in a median.

Milestones are alternatively known as mile markers or mileposts (sometimes abbreviated MPs). Mileage is the distance along the road from a fixed commencement point from one-mile marker to the next.

Milestones are installed to provide reference points along the road. This can be used to reassure travelers that the proper path is being followed, and to indicate either distance traveled or the remaining distance to a destination.

Such references are also used by maintenance engineers and emergency services to direct them to specific points where their presence is required.

This term is sometimes used to denote a location even if no physical sign is present. This is useful for accident reporting or other record keeping.

Surveyors place milestones to mark the boundaries between the jurisdictions separated by borders.

When I think of jurisdictions and boundaries, I think of the thresholds I went through, those seasons in my life when there was great pain and the seasons of great joy and increase. There were many milestones in my life where I went to another level of revelation and demonstration.

As I encountered these milestones I could sense and see the boundaries change in my life that moved me into jurisdictions that gave me greater power and authority to operate in on behalf of the government of the Kingdom of God.

Clarity To My Identity And Purpose

These milestones brought greater clarity on who I was, my identity in Christ and the authority I had as a believer. They helped me come into alignment, make the necessary adjustments with God's government, plans and purposes for my life so I could flow in God's power and authority.

As you read this book each chapter will reflect an area of my life where I came into greater clarity, understanding and wisdom on how to receive and grow in all that God had planned for me. I not only received and grew in these areas for myself personally but learned how to move in God's power and authority to minister in miracles, signs and wonders for others.

Experiences, Encounters Became Milestones

Here are a few experiences, encounters, and milestones I went through that set the course for my journey.

Milestone: As a teenager, I went to church to please my mother; it was more going through religious motions than a relationship with Jesus. When I went to church it was more of a religious experience, I knew the mechanics, and I knew the lingo, but I had no relationship with the Lord. I saw powerful moves of God in people's lives but never experienced it for myself. I knew it was real, I experienced great conviction, the pulling of the Holy Spirit, but I was not ready to make the commitment.

Even though I made no commitment, that was a milestone in my life where things were recorded but I did not see the sign at that time. Seeds were planted that grew and later produced fruit.

A Messed-Up Life Surrendered To Jesus

Milestone: When I married Nancy, I told her, "When we have children we will go to church and serve the Lord." We waited a little longer then we should have. We were about five years into our marriage living in the Philippines where I was serving in the U.S. Air Force at Clark Air Force Base.

Our lives were a mess, I was drinking heavily daily and Nancy and I were pretty much living separate lives. I was involved in an aircraft rodeo competition and we won first place in the Southeast Asian theater, so this gave our squadron an opportunity to compete in the United States. We took a C-130 around the world, competed with 31 squadrons and took third place.

After the competition I took some leave and went home to visit my mum and family. Every time I would go home my mother always had me promise I would go to church with her. So, the Sunday I was there I kept my promise and went to church.

I cannot remember what the preacher preached but I was under so much conviction, the Holy Spirit was pulling on me so strong to make a commitment and surrender my life to Jesus Christ. I made a deal with the Lord and said, "As soon as I get back to the Philippines I will go to church and surrender my life to You."

When I got back to the Philippines, I gave Nancy a beautiful watch I had bought in Japan and she said, "I will take the watch, but I want a divorce." I told her, "You can do whatever you want but I am going to church this Sunday."

Sunday, July 1, 1979, Nancy, and I went to an Assembly of God missionary church pastored by Gene and Heather Burgess, outside Friendship Gate, Clark Air Base where I was stationed. We surrendered our lives to Jesus and never looked back. That decision, that day was a major milestone in our lives.

The Importance Of Application

Right from the very beginning we realized the importance of understanding and applying God's Word and having that intimacy with the

Holy Spirit. The revelation of the foundation I have built upon all these years, the foundation of my relationship with Jesus through intimacy with the Holy Spirit and God's Word is so important.

If we are not building our relationship with Father God on a solid foundation then there will be a day when things will crumble, and we will be standing in a pile of rubble and have to start all over again.

I will share a little more on the importance of a solid foundation in another chapter.

All of who I am and what I do comes from knowing Father God's heart, through my understanding, application of God's Word, and listening to that small still voice called the Holy Spirit. I have learned how to walk with a now word for a now season.

Bull Story

Milestone: Another major milestone in my life that was a catalyst for the healing ministry I have today was when I was attacked and gored by a 2,500 lb. bull. I was working on a dairy farm milking 375 cows twice a day.

On a Saturday morning as I was in a pole barn working, bringing the cows into the milking parlor I heard a noise behind me, so I turned around and it was a 2,500-pound Holstein bull on a dead run towards me. I look to see where I could go, and I saw a feeder bin I could jump into where the bull couldn't get me. As I stepped out to run for the feeder bin I slipped and fell. When I got up, the bull had his head in my back pushing me into a large pole crushing my back and face. I fell back on the ground and the bull kept hitting me, throwing me into the air. I could hear my clothes and flesh ripping. I was thrown as high as nine feet at least seven times.

As I was going through this, I came out of my body. I was looking down watching myself being torn apart by this beast. Then, suddenly I heard these words come out of my mouth, "Lord spare my life," and immediately the bull stopped and walked clear down to the other end of the barn.

That day I had an out of body experience. I believe I died, came out of my body and was looking down at myself being mauled and torn apart by this beast. I told Nancy I felt like I got ripped off after reading about other people's experiences that died and came out of their body, went to heaven, and saw Jesus. I never left the barn! I was just hanging around the rafters.

Compassion For Those In Pain

Because of that encounter with that bull, for the next year I experienced severe pain due to a cracked sternum in three places, a gored hip and several cracked and broken bones in my rib cage, and two ribs broken off my rib cage.

Because of the extreme pain I encountered it gave me compassion for others in pain. I believe the reason why I move in healing the way I do today is because of what I had experienced with the personal pain in my own life. This was a major milestone in my life!

Each chapter in this book will reveal life's lessons of milestones I reached, thresholds, breakthroughs, and levels I went through to get to where I am today.

Boundaries

When I was looking at the definition of a milestone, I also noticed another word used in a similar way, boundary markers. Boundary markers are a way of imposing human social, financial, physical, and spiritual meanings, and limits on a once undifferentiated environment.

Boundary markers are linked to social hierarchies and they derive their meaning from the authority of a group or person to declare the limits of a given space of land or air way for political, social, or spiritual reasons. Determining who can use this space and its purpose has major implications.

Boundary markers and milestones have been used to mark critical points in history and in one's life.

I will dedicate several chapters of this book dealing with a religious mindset to shifting to a Kingdom mindset and taking territory. Jesus is, The Anointed One, The King of kings and He is all about taking territory.

The Importance Of The Journey

We all have a journey; God has a plan and purpose for our lives. There are many doors to go through, stairs and mountains to climb and roads to go down.

If we have the right foundation, understanding, and knowing the limitless One that lives inside us we will grow and experience the manifest presence of God on this earth.

The premise of this book is to show individuals how to position themselves to receive the supernatural and minister in the supernatural or both.

I do this by taking each milestone, each event, encounter, experience, and revelation and turn it into a lesson for a now application.

Milestones to the Miraculous, is a textbook on how to receive and flow in miracles, signs, wonders, deliverance, and empowerment. That is the Kingdom of God being manifested on this earth!

Chapter 2
Alignment For The Miraculous

Life Experience

As a teenager I joined the U. S. Air Force in 1973 and off I went to boot camp, what a shock. The first statement I heard was we own you the next four years and we are here to help you become a man and a soldier. They continued, we will provide everything you need; clothes, food, housing everything. We are here to change your thinking and your behavior. We are here to help you come into alignment with the U.S. government's way of doing things. We are here to change your culture.

In a nutshell they did not care about my past or what I thought because they were about to train and equip me with everything, they felt I needed to be what they wanted me to be. They took me through the physical disciplines and the mental disciplines. They were shaping every part of my being into a soldier/airman for the U.S. government.

It is amazing what can happen in eight weeks when you are in a sterile environment totally committed to changing you and you being totally committed to being changed. In those eight weeks it was nothing but intense discipline, understanding authority and how to submit to that authority. At the end of those eight weeks I was a changed man committed to serving my government.

After leaving boot camp, I went to tech school, where I was trained in several areas. This is where I was taught the history of the Air Force and its superiority around the world. There is no greater feeling then knowing you are backed by the superiority of the U.S. Air Force. I was taught the chain of command and proper alignment and protocol. I was taught specifically in my career trade. As I was trained and equipped in my trade, I went through several levels: 3 level, 5 level and 7 level.

Each level I gained greater knowledge and greater skills and as I became proficient at that level I moved to the next level. Each level I moved into I had greater responsibility and greater authority. As I went through these levels it was amazing how much more influence and respect, I had at each level. There was always a drive in me to want more.

Foundation

When I look at the definition of foundation it talks about load bearing, something to build upon. A solid foundation can withstand the storms, the weight and stress of the environment. In order to have a solid foundation that can withstand the weight of a life or ministry that glorifies the Lord it takes a deep commitment, investing in core principles and values that become the cornerstone of everything you think about, everything you do.

We must understand that for anyone or anything to be successful it takes commitment.

Commitment Scriptures

Commit your way to the Lord, trust also in Him, and He will do it. (Psalm 37:5 NASB)

Open up before God, keep nothing back; he'll do whatever needs to be done: He'll validate your life in the clear light of day and stamp you with approval at high noon. (Psalm 37:5, 6 Message)

I have fought the good fight, I have finished the course, I have kept the faith. (2 Tim 4:7 NASB)

Be diligent to present yourself approved to God as a workman who does not need to be ashamed, accurately handling the word of truth. (2 Tim 2:15 NASB)

You shall love the Lord your God with all your heart and with all your soul and with all your might. (Deut. 6:5 NASB)

Look at the commitment Jesus made for us. He gave it all so we might have life and life abundantly.

The thief comes only to steal and kill and destroy; I came that they may have life and have it abundantly. (John 10:10 NASB)

Lessons Learned

There are a lot of great lessons we can apply here. One thing that we must be careful of as we move from glory to glory, faith to faith is that our motive is right.

First, we must understand that when we become born again our citizenship, commitment and loyalty is to the King of Kings. We are now committed to the Kingdom of God and its government. If we seek first the Kingdom of God and His righteousness, He will take care of our clothes, food, housing and much more. We must learn to come into alignment with the Kingdom of God and its culture.

Second, our past is behind us and we are new creatures in Christ Jesus. Now we are going to be trained and equipped according to Ephesians.

And He gave some as apostles, and some as prophets, and some as evangelists, and some as pastors and teachers, for the equipping of the saints for the work of service, to the building up of the body of Christ; until we all attain to the unity of the faith, and of the knowledge of the Son of God, to a mature man, to the measure of the stature which belongs to the fullness of Christ. (Ephesians 4:11-13 NASB)

This is where we must be even more committed and loyal to this government, the Kingdom of God allowing those in authority to change our thinking which will, in turn change our behavior. Jesus was totally committed to provide everything we need, and we should be totally committed to being discipled and equipped to be everything He wants us to be.

Third, we must understand government order and alignment. What is the role of our leaders, specifically what is the role of an apostle? As an emerging sent one or a mature apostle we must go through different levels, each level releasing greater responsibility, greater authority, and greater power, this is true discipleship. There are many things that an apostle does, but I will just focus on a couple. I function as an Apostle, so this is important for me and for those who are emerging into the apostolic. If you embrace the great commission as a sent one, you need to understand this.

Apostle – Sent One

Apostle means a sent one, God the Father sent His Son Jesus, who was the Chief Apostle with full backing, authority, and resources. The Holy Spirit was sent to empower, lead and guide us, God's word was sent to save, heal, deliver and so much more. Jesus raised up apostles and sent them and we have been given the great commission to go out and be the salt and light.

An apostle is called, empowered, and sent to tear down the existing government, the gates of hades, the realm of darkness and establish the Kingdom of God. An apostle teaches proper alignment and order. Proper alignment and order remove the barriers and allows for the manifest presence of God to come forth. Proper alignment also brings greater revelation and the awareness of Holy Spirit in us and the tools and weapons at our disposal.

How I Came Into Moving In The Miraculous

Over the years as I have ministered, pastors and leaders have asked how I came into moving in miracles, signs and wonders and the one main thing that I learned in the military and carried over into the ministry was the importance authority. There is no greater feeling then knowing that you are backed by almighty God, far greater than any kingdom or government on this earth. It is a wonderful feeling moving in the power of the Holy Spirit.

Illustration On Resistance

One of my trades in the Air Force was aircraft electronics and I learned how dimmer switches worked. The more resistance you put into a circuit the less the power would flow, the less resistance the more power. When we come into apostolic alignment and order we get the resistance out of our thinking and we operate according to the mind of Christ and divine order, thus moving in greater revelation, authority, and power.

Where Does Our Authority Come From
How Do We Move In It

Where does our authority come from and how do we move in that authority? There are several things we need to look at to understand and walk with confident authority. The best place to start is with the Master, Jesus.

Jesus gave them this answer, "Very truly I tell you, the Son can do nothing by himself; he can do only what he sees his Father doing, because whatever the Father does the Son also does. (John 5:19 NIV)

By myself I can do nothing; I judge only as I hear, and my judgment is just, for I seek not to please myself but him who sent me. (John 5:30 NIV)

For I did not speak on My own initiative, but the Father Himself who sent Me has given Me a commandment as to what to say and what to speak. (John 12:49 NASB)

Jesus is clearly showing us that He was under the authority of the Father, He said, I only do and say what He wants. It is so important that we understand this first and foremost. If we are not under authority, we have no authority.

Sons Of Sceva Vs The Centurion Soldier

Seven sons of one Sceva, a Jewish chief priest, were doing this. And the evil spirit answered and said to them, "I recognize Jesus, and I know about Paul, but who are you?" And the man, in whom was the evil spirit, leaped on them and subdued all of them and overpowered them, so that they fled out of that house naked and wounded. (Acts 19:14-16 NASB)

The sons of Sceva were considered vagabonds, not planted anywhere or under anyone's authority. Because they were not under authority, they had no authority. The demons said we recognize Jesus and Paul because they were under authority, but who are you.

The centurion on the other hand clearly understood what it was to come under authority.

And when Jesus entered Capernaum, a centurion came to Him, imploring Him, 6 and saying, "Lord, my servant is lying paralyzed at home, fearfully tormented." Jesus *said to him, "I will come and heal him." But the centurion said, "Lord, I am not worthy for You to come under my roof, but just say the word, and my servant will be healed. For I also am a man under authority, with soldiers under me; and I say to this one, 'Go!' and he goes, and to another, 'Come!' and he comes, and to my slave, 'Do this!' and he does it." Now when Jesus heard this, He marveled and said to those who were following, "Truly I say to you, I have not found such great faith with anyone in Israel. I say to you that many will come from east and west, and recline at the table with Abraham, Isaac and Jacob in the kingdom of heaven; but the sons of the kingdom will be cast out into the outer darkness; in that place there will be weeping and gnashing of teeth." And Jesus said to the centurion, "Go; it shall be done for you as you have believed." And the servant was healed that very moment. (Matt 8:5-13 NASB)

Look at the difference; just say the word, now that is understanding authority!

Flesh Vs Spirit

We are talking about Kingdom of God authority. Paul talks about this even in dealing with our fleshly walk. But if God himself has taken up residence in your life, you can hardly be thinking more of yourself than of him. Anyone, of course, who has not welcomed this invisible but clearly present God, the Spirit of Christ, will not know what we are talking about. But for you who welcome him, in whom he dwells—even though you still experience all the limitations of sin—you yourself experience life on God's terms. It stands to reason, doesn't it, that if the alive-and-present God who raised Jesus from the dead moves into your life, he'll do the same thing in you that he did in Jesus, bringing you alive to himself? When God lives and breathes in you (and he does, as surely as he did in Jesus), you are delivered from that dead life. With his Spirit living in you, your body will be as alive as Christ's! (Rom. 8:9-11 Message)

Spirit Of Christ
Government Of God

Christ is not Jesus last name; it is a function. The literal meaning of the name Christ is Anointed One, but the practical meaning is Inaugurated One (King). When we see the Spirit of Christ, we see King, Kingdom of God, God's government. We live and conduct our lives on God's terms, according to the government of God. What is the government of God? It is rule, reign, dominion, and authority. When we truly have the Spirit of Christ in us, we are saying He is King, and the Kingdom of God is within me and it has rule, reign, dominion, and authority.

Mind, Will And Emotions

Where and how is that authority directed? Christ the King lives in our spirit. When we ask Christ to come into our lives the Holy Spirit comes and lives in our spirit and governs us, He does it in the soul part of our being. Our soul is made up of mind, will and emotions. This is where our thinking, decision making, and feelings operate. This is where we submit and come under the authority of the government of God. The Spirit of Christ (Government of God) has rule, reign, dominion and authority over our thinking, decision making and feelings.

Paul talks about the conflict of two natures in Romans, I do not understand what I do. For what I want to do I do not do, but what I hate I do. (Romans 7:15 NIV) Paul is talking about his struggle with the flesh and he gives the answer to the problem, we need the Spirit of Christ in us. However, you are not in the flesh but in the Spirit, if indeed the Spirit of God dwells in you. But if anyone does not have the Spirit of Christ, he does not belong to Him. (Romans 8:9 NASB)

We either submit to the flesh and let it have rule, reign, dominion and authority or we submit to the Spirit of Christ, the government of God. When we come under the authority of the Kingdom of God, we have authority and power from the Kingdom of God.

14

Delegated Authority

So, Jesus said to them again, "Peace be to you; just as the Father has sent Me, I also send you." (John 20:21 NASB)

Jesus says, "Truly, truly I say unto you, he who believes in Me, the works that I do, he will do also; and greater works then these he will do; because I go to be with the Father." (John 14:12 NASB)

Jesus submitted to and came under authority and that is why He had authority and that is the example He has given us. Jesus was sent under authority and we must go under authority to have authority.

Submit therefore to God. But resist the devil, and he will flee from you. (James 4:7 NASB)

A Key To Moving In Miracles, Signs, And Wonders

One of the greatest keys to moving in miracles, sign and wonders is, understanding the authority you have as a believer, knowing where that authority comes from and where it is directed. When we come into alignment, everything changes.

There is always going to be a conflict between the two natures: the flesh and the spirit. Which one is going to win on any given day?

Story Of Two Dogs

I heard a story of a man from Alaska that had two dogs, one German Shepherd and one Doberman Pincher. Every Saturday he would take the dogs into town and let the dogs fight and while the dogs are fighting, people are placing bets, even the owner, on which dog will win.

Three weeks in a row the German Shepherd wins, then the next two weeks the Doberman Pincher wins, then the German Shepherd. One guy noticed that the owner won every time. He went to the owner and said, I see you win every time, how do you know which dog is going to win. He said, that's easy, the one I feed the most. *Author unknown*

It Is Our Choice

Every day we have a choice, feed our flesh or our spirit. Submit to the flesh or submit to the Spirit of Christ, the government of God and let it have rule, reign, dominion, and authority over our mind, will and emotions. These choices will determine whether we will move in Kingdom authority, move in miracles, signs, and wonders. When the flesh gets out of the way the glory of God, His manifest presence will come forth and we will experience the miraculous. This is done by submitting to the Word of God and that small still voice called, Holy Spirit.

But the eleven disciples proceeded to Galilee, to the mountain which Jesus had designated. When they saw Him, they worshiped Him; but some were doubtful. And Jesus came up and spoke to them, saying, "All authority has been given to Me in heaven and on earth. Go therefore and make disciples of all the nations, baptizing them in the name of the Father and the Son and the Holy Spirit, teaching them to observe all that I commanded you; and lo, I am with you always, even to the end of the age." (Matt. 28:16-20 NASB)

Jesus is saying, all authority has been given to us in heaven and on earth and He is telling us to go. We are being sent with apostolic authority; the same authority Jesus was sent with. We may not all fill the office of an Apostle, but we are called to be sent with an apostolic anointing. When we are doing the Father's will, we have full backing of the Father and all His resources available. The greater the revelation of this and the more we came into apostolic alignment, the more authority and power we will move in.

My Personal Experience

As I move in ministry I declare and demonstrate God's word. I speak to pain to leave in Jesus name and it leaves, I speak to hernias and tumors to leave in Jesus name and they leave, I speak to bones to come together in Jesus name and they come together. I speak to depression and anxiety to leave in Jesus name and they leave. I am seeing an amazing consistency in the authority I operate in. I say this not to brag on myself, but I do know who I am in Christ and the authority I have as a sent one. I have learned how to come into apostolic alignment and stay in apostolic alignment.

16

It Is For You

The exciting thing about the above statement is that it is for all who accept the Great Commission, all who come into apostolic alignment with the Kingdom of God. I challenge you to believe and embrace your call as a sent one and move out in the miraculous.

I will go into this in more depth in future chapters.

Chapter 3
Your God Given Purpose

Where there is no vision [no revelation of God and His word], the people are unrestrained; But happy and blessed is he who keeps the law [of God]. (Prov. 29:18 Amp)

If people cannot see what God is doing, they stumble all over themselves, when they attend to what He reveals they are most blessed. (Prov. 29:18 Message)

When you have no vision, you have no boundaries, no direction, no purpose. You are moved by circumstances, feelings, you are pulled this way one day and that way the next. You cannot see beyond your circumstances.

Vision is like a compass it keeps you on course, steady, moving forward, planted, producing fruit.

God Has A Plan

For I know the plans I have for you, "declares the Lord, "plans to prosper you and not to harm you, plans to give you hope and a future. (Jeremiah 29:11 NIV)

"Before I formed you in the womb, I knew you, before you were born I set you apart; I appointed you as a prophet to the nations." (Jeremiah 1:5 NIV)

You were born for the role God has planned for you.

Then the Lord answered me and said, "Write down the vision and inscribe it clearly on the tablets, So that one who reads it may run. (Habakkuk 2:2 NASB)

Just as the Son of man did not come to be served, but to serve, and to give His life as a ransom for many. (Matt 20:28 NASB)

Ask God to bring clarity of purpose. Why do you exist?

As a Dream Coach, I help people establish two-word purpose

statements.

We exist to serve! My two-word purpose statement is: I exist to serve other by, Empowering Expectation. Our ministry, Bridge to Destiny Ministry exist to serve others by Bridging Destiny.

One of the most important things in life is, knowing your purpose.

Every day as I meet with people, churches, and businesses I am empowering their expectations and bridging their destiny by connecting them to Biblical principles, the right people, and resources.

Clarity Of Purpose

Here in Jeremiah we see a moment of clarity.

This is what the Lord says: "Stand at the crossroads and look; ask for the ancient paths, ask where the good way is, and walk in it, and you will find rest for your souls. (Jeremiah 6: 16 NIV)

Like many verses in the Bible it is filled with practical wisdom.

It is, first, a word from the Lord, and as in all communication, there is one who speaks and one who listens, and so it is important that we listen.

Thus, says the Lord. God is speaking to a time and a place, and Jeremiah, one of the great prophets of God recorded this.

What are the crossroads? The crossroads are those moments and places of decision.

Our destiny is so important, clarity is so important for a now time in a now season.

We have been at the crossroads many times, wondering which way to turn. We came to a place and a moment of decision.

Look around. Consider. The seeing and reflecting may lead us to ask the question:

Am I going in the right direction? What is the ancient path?

Well, it is not the next thing, not always the relevant thing or the newest gadget or program.

The ancient path was identified when Jesus said to Thomas, "I am the way, and the truth, and the life; no one comes to the Father but through me." (John 14:6 NASB)

The way means "to do it the way Jesus did it, by becoming absolutely needy and dependent on the Father".

There are so many people at the crossroads wondering what is my, God given purpose? Why do I exist? I believe if readers of this book will get ahold of these principles and apply them, they will be right in the middle of God's will, walking in the favor of God.

I have found that the greater clarity I have, the more intentional I am.

Being Intentional

For a Christian, living intentionally begins with living a life submitted to Christ. In Christ we find our identity and purpose.

"Trust in the Lord with all your heart and lean not on your own understanding; in all your ways submit to him, and he will make your paths straight." (Proverbs 3:5-6 NIV)

Knowing your purpose is key because your purpose determines your priorities. As you seek God, He will reveal your specific calling and purpose to you.

Intentional living means to live on purpose or to live deliberately with an aim or a plan.

Discover your purpose, prioritize areas of that purpose, establish strategies, set goals, and action steps so you can be intentional with God's purpose for your life.

Favor Of God On Your Purpose

For You bless the righteous person, Lord, You surround him with favor as with a shield. (Psalms 5:12 NASB)

What exactly does favor do? Favor is the affection of God towards you that releases an influence through you so that other people are inclined to like, trust, and cooperate with you.

Favor is a magnet to the blessing and promotion of God. Favor, however, is always attached to a purpose and comes with a price. You could say that favor is more on the assignment than the person.

God wraps a flesh and blood servant around the assignment He favors. If you quit the assignment, the favor will go to the person God raises up to pick up the assignment.

Look at Joseph's life, the scripture says in Genesis 39, the Lord was with him and Joseph found favor several times. Joseph stayed true to his dream through false accusations and being treated badly. Joseph forgave them, continued in his purpose and his dream was fulfilled.

God's favor operates in your life as you work out the service, He has called you into. Things start going right, divine appointments abound, and people come to you to join your cause.

The first mention of favor in the New Testament is in Luke. Here Mary is approached by Gabriel, whose salutation heralds Mary's favored status in the throne room. Notice in these verses that the word 'favor' is repeated twice. Favor, "charis" (pronounced khar-ece), is a word revealing a two-fold operation of the law of attraction. The first definition describes an attraction of God to you and the second describes the release of an influence through you that inclines other people to trust, like and assist you in your assignment. (Luke 1:28-31 NASB)

Do you remember Job's confession, that God gave him "life and favor" by his "visitation? (Job 10:12 KJV) "Here in Mary's life we see exactly how this applies. God is attracted to her because of her heart's desire toward Him.

Likewise, He comes to visit you. When He comes to visit you, He leaves you different from before He came.

In Mary's case, she was left pregnant! God reveals that in addition to His many names of the Old Testament, Jehovah Rophi and Jehovah Nisi, etc., He is also Jehovah Sneaky! When He visits you, He impregnates you with a vision, an assignment, and a mission.

You may not understand it all at first, but once the favor of God comes, the assignment becomes more personal and compelling.

When you spend prolonged time in God's presence it is natural that at some point you conceive His desire.

In fact, the word "Desire" in Latin is a two-part word De: "of", and Sire: "Father". Literally, desire is "of the father." You were designed with a spiritual womb that is capable of birthing God's purposes.

God's hand of favor will guide us through the fog of uncertainty.

Developing A Kingdom Mindset
To Walk Out His Purpose In Your Life

For me to understand who I am in Christ Jesus and my purpose, I need to understand God's plan and purpose for mankind. God's plan is to establish His Kingdom through His Son Jesus Christ. Jesus came to this earth died on the cross, rose on the third day, ascended to heaven and is sitting at the right hand of the Father.

Through Christ's works:

He established the Kingdom of God

He restored all that was lost in the Garden

He established His church on the day of Pentecost

He delegated His authority to the believer.

ECCLESIA

One important area of authority we need to understand and operate in is Ecclesia. And I say unto you that you are Peter, and upon this rock I will build my church; and the gates of Hades will not overpower it. I will give you the keys of the kingdom of heaven; and whatever you bind on earth shall be bound in heaven, and whatever you loose on earth shall have been loosed in heaven. (Matt 16:18,19 NASB) That word church is ecclesia.

We are called from the world into the Kingdom of God when we become born again, and we are called out of our homes to assemble. The called out to assemble is Ecclesia. Ecclesia is a group called out of their homes within the Kingdom to assemble before the King on behalf of His government, His rule and reign, His will, and His ways.

The Ecclesia is not about a place or building, it can be at a place or building where the group assembles but it is the group assembled that is the Ecclesia.

When these citizens of the Kingdom come out to assemble, they serve at the pleasure of the King and His government.

Therefore, having a Kingdom mindset is so important, we must understand Kingdom culture, protocol, systems, and strategies.

Kingdom thinking and Kingdom way needs to be in our Commerce, our Socialization, our Education our Health our Culture our Process, and our Stewardship

I will get into the Kingdom in greater depth in future chapters.

God's plan and purpose for the believer is to continue to declare, demonstrate and establish the Kingdom of God until He, the King of Kings returns.

God's plan and purpose is our mandate. It is so important to get this information, walk in the experience of it through application and see the transformation in your life and the lives of others.

Chapter 4
Your Identity In Christ

Where there is no vision [no revelation of God and His word], the people are unrestrained; But happy and blessed is he who keeps the law [of God]. (Prov. 29:18 AMP)

If people can't see what God is doing, they stumble all over themselves; But when they attend to what He reveals they are most blessed. (Prov. 29:18 MESSAGE)

When there is no vision there are no boundaries, no direction, and purpose. You are moved by circumstances, feelings, you are pulled this way one day and that way the next. You cannot see beyond your circumstances.

Vision is like a compass it keeps you on course, steady, moving forward, planted, producing fruit.

For I know the plans I have for you, "declares the Lord," plans to prosper you, not to harm you, plans to give you hope and a future. (Jer. 29:11 NIV)

God has a plan and purpose for every one of us. It is so important to know who we are in Christ Jesus and the authority we have as a believer

It does not matter what we have gone through, Jesus brings restoration out of destruction.

The Box

As I went through life there was always someone trying to identify me, trying to put me in their box. I can look back through my life and see the different seasons, and how I tried to conform to the status quo, allowing people to put things on me that did not belong. I think of Saul trying to put his armor on David.

I thank God for people like Sandy Kulkin, the developer of the DISC personality profile. This profile clearly defines the four major personalities and their characteristics. This helped me so much not only in knowing that I was normal but there were others out there like me. I was an off the charts high D and according to all the personality profiles the percentage of people that test in this category are extremely low.

I not only took the profile test but also took the certification to read the results of other profiles so I could help others identify their personalities so they would have a better understanding of how God made them. We must be so careful to not allow circumstances and others establish our identity.

Even in presidential elections I would hear media say how important it was for one political group to establish their opponent's identity before their opponent had a chance to.

The point I want to make here is how important it is to know who you are in Christ Jesus. There are so many scriptures speaking of your identity and how the Lord sees you.

For you created my inmost being, you knit me together in my mother's womb. I praise you because I am fearfully and wonderfully made; your works are wonderful; I know that full well. (Psalm 139:13,14 NIV)

For we are God's workmanship, created in Christ Jesus to do good works, which God prepared in advance for us to do. (Ephesians 2:10 NIV)

Therefore, if anyone is in Christ, this person is a new creation; the old things passed away; behold new things have come. (2 Corinthians 5:17 NASB)

When we come into the Kingdom of God, we begin to realize who made us and discover our new family. Our old life is behind us and we have a new future in Christ Jesus, King of kings and Lord of lords. In this realization our perception of who we are changes. We need to believe God's Word and what it says about us:

- We are fearfully and wonderfully made, and we are God's workmanship.

- We are created in Christ Jesus.

- We have an inheritance; we have all the resources of heaven and earth at our disposal to accomplish what Father God has assigned.

Branding Process

As I was going through a new branding process after having resigned from pastoring, I began to hear the Lord speaking to me about how many of His children have been rustled like cattle. They have been taken down and branded. They may have been branded by the devil, by circumstances, by being a victim, or by failures. Its other people putting their brand on you. The Lord is saying I have a plan and a purpose I have my mark, my assignment.

In understanding our identity, we must understand our purpose. So many Christians only understand, I am saved, I have escaped hell and I am going to heaven. They are waiting for that to happen and their purpose is to hang on the best they can until that day comes.

That is what is called The Gospel of Salvation, basically this says that I am saved to get to heaven and if I can take a few with me, wonderful. But in most cases people are not overly concerned about evangelizing.

Works Of Jesus Christ

For me to understand who I am in Christ Jesus I need to understand God's plan and purpose for mankind. God's plan is to establish His Kingdom through His Son, Jesus Christ. Jesus came to this earth, died on the cross, rose on the third day, ascended to heaven and is sitting at the right hand of the Father.

Through Christ's works:

- He established the Kingdom of God

- He restored all that was lost in the Garden

- He established His church on the day of Pentecost

- He delegated His authority to the believer.

Declare – Demonstrate - Establish

God's plan and purpose for the believer is to continue to declare, demonstrate and establish the Kingdom of God until He, the King of kings returns. We do this through salvations, miracles, signs, wonders, deliverance, and empowerment.

Because I am a high D personality, and I believe in this mandate so much, it has kept me in hot water a good part of my ministry life. Even though I have pastored for 25 years I really did not fit the pastoral profile but at that time I saw no other options. The pastoral profile is to care for, comfort and manage the sheep. I cared about the sheep and comforted them through major crisis in their lives, but I was not about keeping people in their present condition. I was always challenging the status quo by attempting to get people to see their potential and to move them into their destiny.

I always loved my congregation, cared about their future and was willing to take the grief of offending someone if it meant moving them forward in their destiny.

I am a future oriented person, so letting go of my past and moving into my future is important. So often people would come to me and want me to be more pastoral and just go with the flow. I tried it and it almost killed me. Even though I had people trying to put me in their box I had leaders around me for years telling me, "you're apostolic, you have an apostolic anointing, you're an apostle." I fought that for years because it was not acceptable with the group I was with. I do not believe you have to be pastoral to lead a church, but I do believe that if you are not pastoral, then you need to have pastoral care ministry in your church.

Pastors Comfort The Afflicted
Apostles Afflict The Comfortable

Through the years I came more and more into my true call and identity, I had greater clarity on my assignment and purpose. My last 10 years of pastoring I transitioned into an apostolic role of leadership establishing five-fold ministries within the church and outside of the church. I truly felt, and still feel, that I am to equip the sheep to do the work of the ministry. (Ephesians 4:11)

Whether you are leading a group from a pastoral or apostolic perspective people have a certain opinion of who you should be, and how you, your wife and children should act. For many if you do not fit in their box they leave and go somewhere else to find someone who will fit in their box.

It was always painful to have a family or an individual come to me and tell me they are leaving the church; it was almost like someone asking you for a divorce. I spent many days and nights in my office or bed weeping over those that left the church because I saw so much potential in them. When new people came in from another church in the community, I could feel the pain of the pastor they left.

Pentecostal, charismatic, spirit filled people are more nomadic then most other groups. I believe it is because of the emotional side of being spirit-filled, too often their feeling overrides the fact of what God's Word says.

Feelings are important but we must be grounded and rooted to produce good fruit. Just when you think someone is about to produce good fruit, they uproot themselves and go somewhere else. Why am I saying this? Because it can mess with your identity as a leader if you do not know who you are in Christ and your purpose in The Kingdom.

I Am Normal

One of the milestones for me was when I saw I was normal, and God made me this way for a purpose. I always had a confidence; it was part of my makeup but when I brought that confidence into alignment with my identity in Christ it all started coming together. I began to see greater consistency, authority, and fruit in my ministry.

Like I said I had confidence that I was born again and had a call of God and had the basics, but I did not have the revelation, wisdom, knowledge and understanding I have today.

Submitting Is So Important

You need to understand I am not talking about being a lone ranger or going rouge. It is not about being rebellious, it is about being obedient. I have a whole teaching dedicated to coming under authority and submitting. I have always surrounded myself with leaders that had wisdom and maturity and I desired to have them speak into my life. By coming into alignment with my identity I found people celebrating and not tolerating what God was speaking to me.

Ministers Network

I have fought hard for my identity. There is so much pressure in some of these denominations wanting you to think and act like them. Fifteen years ago, I started a ministers' network and two of the major aspects of the network are: it is relational not positional, and we chose to celebrate instead of tolerating. Those two aspects changed everything for so many. Nancy and I love serving and celebrating these ministers.

I even had to defend my biological name Burpee growing up. Being 5 foot 7 with the last name Burpee and going through the public-school system was not easy. I was in the principal's office more then I wanted to be. I was kicked off the bus and even kicked out of the fifth grade for fighting, mostly being teased about my last name. I even had two ladies try to drown me in a brook for fighting with their son. One of these ladies came to our house and knocked on the door and my father answered, and the lady went off on my father telling him what I had done. Just before she left, she told my dad, "Your son is a born leader he is just leading them in the wrong direction." I was not innocent in some of these fights I developed a chip on my shoulder. I am proud of my name and it is part of my heritage and identity.

I will tell you this, I am proud to be who I am in Christ and I am proud to carry the Burpee name. The name I fought for is now on marquees, websites, social media platforms and books because I would not allow someone else determine my identity.

He made Him who knew no sin to be sin in our behalf, so that we might become the righteousness of God in Him. (2 Cor. 5:21 NASB)

Steal – Kill – Destroy

The Devil is another area of focus when it comes to our identity. The thief comes only to steal and kill and destroy; I came so that they would have life and have it abundantly. (John 10:10 NASB)

For I know the plans that I have for you, 'declares the Lord, 'plans for prosperity and not for disaster, to give you a future and a hope. (Jer. 29:11 NASB)

God has a plan and a purpose for every one of us. It is so important that we know who we are in Christ Jesus and the authority we have as a believer. It does not matter what we have gone through, Jesus brings restoration out of destruction.

Steal – your identity, by bringing confusion into your life so you do not know who you are.

If you must go to others for validation, the enemy has stolen your identity.

If you seek purpose and direction in others, you are not seeking the source, Jesus Christ.

Pro Football Player

A good friend of mine was a pro football player for years, that was all he knew, that was his identity. He sustained a major injury and was released from playing pro football. This was devastating to him; he went into depression and had a difficult time. He then had some people minister to him and help him come to a place where he knew who he was in Christ, he knew his purpose and he knew he had the authority to carry it out. This man had a major healing ministry and led thousands to Christ. There are multitudes struggling with their identity and maybe this book will help.

Delete – Delete - Delete

She had arthritis and fibromyalgia. At a young age this woman was molested by her father over several years in three different homes.

We had ministered to her in the morning service and she could not get her healing. She told us about the unforgiveness and bitterness she had towards her dad who had died several years before. Nancy had lunch with her and told her she needed to talk to the Lord about forgiving her dad and letting go of the bitterness.

That afternoon she had a vision where she saw herself sitting at a computer hitting a delete button in every room where she had been molested. After deleting the last room in each house, the house collapsed. As she was going through the deleting process, she felt the physical pain leaving her body. She came to church that night and was totally healed physically and emotionally. She was set free and not walking in the identity of a victim any longer.

Transformed Life

I was in a meeting and an individual came into the room. It was hard to tell whether they were male or female. This person was a body builder and had their hair pulled back. There was a harshness on their face and tightness in their jaw. It was evident that they had experienced an extremely hard life.

I began to talk about our identity and how the devil and others can steal it, but God does not want us to live there. He wants us to be free and have life abundantly. This person began to share about how she was molested and raped by her father for years. Because of that she lost her identity and was living it through a body builder. I took her by the hands and began to speak the Word of God into her life. I came against the lies the enemy had told her. She came to a place in her heart where she realized that her un-forgiveness and bitterness were hurting her more than the one that hurt her.

She forgave her father of all the hurt, pain, and torment he had put on her. Her sister also had been drugged and raped by their father for years. As she went through this process of forgiving and letting go her countenance literally began to change. The hardness was leaving instantly. She began to come into her real identity. God was setting her free and bringing her into her true identity.

Kill - your desire, by bringing circumstances into your life to distract you from your purpose.

Have you ever had an experience in your life where you made a commitment to God and all of the sudden it seems like everything is falling apart, trouble on the job, loved ones getting sick? You find yourself focusing all your time and energy in resolving the problems, you find yourself tired and exhausted.

Bull Story – In chapter one I told my bull story. I had made a major commitment to get out of the Air Force and go to into full time ministry. Serving God full time was my greatest desire. The devil brought a major distraction trying to kill my desire. It did not work!

Destroy - your spirit

The spirit of a person can endure his sickness, but as for a broken spirit, who can bear it. (Prov 18:14 NASB) A wounded spirit separates you from the love of Christ and all His promises and blessings. The power of Jesus Christ brings restoration out of destruction.

Pastor Hating His Father

This Pastor is preaching the word and God begins to deal with him about his wounded spirit and his hatred for his father. This wounded spirit was on most of his siblings and mother.

God spoke to him to go to his father and ask his father to forgive him of his attitude and hatred toward him. That un-forgiveness was eating the pastor alive. By releasing his father and asking him to forgive him of his attitude towards him totally set that pastor free and he was able to lead his father to Christ and was honored to conduct his father's funeral years later.

That unforgiveness was destroying that pastor's spirit.

There is a divine purpose in all our lives, and we must be persistent and determined to not allow our identity to be stolen, our desires killed, or our spirit destroyed. We cannot not allow any un-forgiveness to be in us, it will keep us from walking in our true identity.

If we do not know who we are in Christ, we will not clearly walk in our assignment.

32

I want to challenge you to let go, forgive, forgiveness will set you free.

Chapter 5
Breaking Off A Religious Spirit 1

What Is A Religious Spirit
How Does It Work

This deceptive force has labored to stop the progress of the Church throughout the ages. Religion is not bad thing when we adhere to the world's literal meaning: to consider divine things. The word "religion" has three meanings in the Word of God: outward religious acts, such as praying and going to church; the feeling of absolute dependence; and the observance of moral law as a divine institution.

Religion is linked to worship. Religion, when pure, is powerful.

However, religion is also defined as an organized system of doctrine with an approved pattern of behavior. This behavior must demonstrate a proper form of worship.

This is where we move from pure and undefiled religion to ritual.

This religious spirit is not just an attitude of religiosity. It is an evil spirit that must be resisted, bound, and cast out.

As members of the Body of Christ we need to know more about this agent of darkness that has deceived both Christians and non-Christians. Why would we want to know more about a high-ranking demon? It is quite simple. As Paul writes, so that no advantage would be taken of us by Satan, for we are not ignorant of his schemes. (2 Corinthians 2:11 NASB)

Turn this around, and it means that if for any reason, we are ignorant of the devices or the wiles of the devil, he will inevitably take advantage of us!

One of our problems is that "spirit of religion" is not a biblical term. You cannot find it in the concordance. That does not imply, of course, that it is not a useful term. When you think of it, you cannot find "Trinity" or "Rapture" or Christmas in the concordance either, just to cite a few examples, but they are good words that we frequently use.

Even the word "religion," by itself appears only two times in the Bible. Once it refers to Judaism (Acts 26:5) and the other simply tells us that true religion, like true faith, is accompanied by works (James 1:26-27).

A Definition Of The "Spirit Of Religion"

The spirit of religion is an agent of Satan assigned to prevent change and to maintain the status quo by using religious devices.

The most radical change recorded in the Bible was the change from the Old Covenant to the New Covenant. When Jesus addressed the disciples of John the Baptist, the last prominent representative of the Old Covenant, He used the terminology "old wineskin" and "new wineskin." (Matthew 9:16-17)

Jesus said that when God has new wine for His people, He pours it only into new wineskins. He does not pour it into old wineskins (which at one time were His new wineskins), because He loves them, and He does not want to destroy them.

The change from an old wineskin to a new wineskin, such as the Apostolic, Five-Fold and the message of the Kingdom of God always meets powerful resistance. However, the resistance does not come from the anointed leaders of the old wineskins.

For instance, John the Baptist blessed the new wineskin saying, He must increase, but I must decrease. (John 3:30 NASB) He said, "He who is coming after me is mightier than I (Matt. 3:11 NASB). Nicodemus and Gamaliel would be other examples of anointed old-wineskin leaders.

The opposition to God's new changes always comes from the unanointed leaders of the old wineskin. For example, the attitude of the Pharisees was the opposite of John the Baptist's attitude. The Pharisees ended up killing Jesus! The last thing they were willing to do was to decrease and thereby lose the position of power that they were enjoying in the old wineskin.

What is going on? I see this as nothing less than the operation of a demonic force of a corporate spirit of religion. It is a device of Satan. We must never be ignorant of his devices.

Four Characteristics Of
The Corporate Spirit Of Religion

If you have been an active believer for some time, chances are that you have come up against the corporate spirit of religion. Consequently, you may recognize these four characteristics.

1. ***The corporate spirit of religion is a high-level demon.*** It is probably on the level of some other principalities that are named in Scripture, such as Wormwood (Rev. 8:11), Beelzebub (Luke 11:15), the prince of Greece (Dan. 10:20) and the queen of heaven (Jeremiah 7:18). Principality is nothing more than a prince over a municipality. That is why the gates of Hades are at the seat of government, the devil wants to control those in power. Jesus has given us Keys of the Kingdom, revelation and strategy to tear down and destroy these gates.

2. ***The corporate spirit of religion invades groups of people, not individuals.*** Spirits that invade individuals, such as a spirit of rejection, a spirit of trauma, a spirit of lust or a personal religious spirit, all need to be cast out of its victims through deliverance ministry.

The assignment of the corporate spirit of religion is collective. It casts a spell over the leaders of whole segments of God's people. This, for example, is reflected in Galatians, O foolish Galatians, who has bewitched you, that ye should not obey the truth, before whose eyes Jesus Christ hath been evidently set forth, crucified among you? (Galatians 3:1 KJV)

That word "bewitched" is a strong word. The Galatians as a whole church were under the spell of the corporate spirit of religion. They hesitated to move into God's new times and seasons for them. In this case the spell, which is a form of curse, needs to be renounced and broken through the blood of Jesus by the spiritual authorities over the group. Then they can be transformed by the renewing of their minds, as it says in Romans 12:2. If they are not willing to do this, the spell will not leave, and the individuals whose minds are renewed will be advised to leave the group.

3. ***The corporate spirit of religion is extremely subtle.*** This spirit does not speak out loud or write on walls or move furniture around the room. People under its influence have no clue to its existence. In

fact, the corporate spirit of religion succeeds in making them think that they are doing God's will! For example, The Pharisees were saying to Him, "Look, why are they doing what is not lawful on the Sabbath? (Mark 2:24 NASB)

Why do your disciples break the traditions of the elders? For they do not wash their hands when they eat bread. (Matthew 15:2 NASB)

The Pharisees had elevated the tradition of the elders into a place equal to Scripture, believing that they were serving God by doing this.

4. *The corporate spirit of religion manipulates leaders into opposing God's plan for new times and seasons.* A good case in point is Peter. When he was with Jesus in Caesarea Philippi, he had one of his best days one morning and one of his worst days the same afternoon. He started off declaring that Jesus was "the Christ, the Son of the living God" (Matthew 16:16 NASB)

Jesus' encouraging response was "Blessed are you, Simon Bar-Jonah, for flesh and blood has not revealed this to you, but My Father who is in heaven" (v.17). That was an awesome day for Peter. But not for long.

Later that same day Jesus told His disciples that He was going to leave them. In other words, times and seasons would change for the disciples. Peter did not like that. He preferred the status quo and he told Jesus so in no uncertain terms.

Look at Jesus' response: "Get behind Me, Satan!" (v. 23). Peter had done a 180 within a matter of hours, and Jesus traced Peter's statement to the realm of darkness. Jesus continued, "You are a stumbling block to Me, for you are not setting your mind on God's purposes, but men's. (v.23).

I do not think it would be stretching things too far to suppose that Satan's agent for making Peter, who was spokesperson for the group, think the wrong way that afternoon, would be the corporate spirit of religion.

Three Principles For Dealing With The Spirit Of Religion

How do those of us that feel that God has assigned us to move into new wineskins deal with the opposition of the spirit of religion?

1. *Do not get sidetracked.* The corporate spirit of religion would love

to weaken you by consuming your time and energy. It frequently uses enticements such as "Let us dialogue" or "We need more prayer" or "Do further study" or "Give the old wineskin another chance." All of this is designed to wear out your mind, the literal meaning of "belah."

2. **Engage in warfare**. Keep in mind that the battle is a spiritual battle, because behind it all, evil spirits are trying to disrupt God's plans. The Bible says, For the weapons of our warfare are not of the flesh, but divinely powerful for the destruction of fortresses. We are destroying arguments and all arrogance raised up against the knowledge of God, and we are taking every thought captive to the obedience of Christ. (2 Corinthians 10:4-5 NASB) We use our spiritual authority through the blood of Christ to bind the corporate spirit of religion, which is trying to make leaders think wrong thoughts.

Many of the resolutions of these conflicts can be resolved with prophetic intercession. This is where we come before the Lord, hear what the Holy Spirit speaks to our spirit concerning these things and we then speak them out as the Holy Spirit guides.

3. **Show your opponent's honor and respect**. Keep in mind that the people who come against you are not your enemies. Your real enemy, the corporate spirit of religion, is simply using certain individuals to accomplish its ungodly desires to maintain the status quo. This is the time to clothe ourselves with humility, as 1 Peter 5:5 tells us to do, because "God resists the proud, but gives grace to the humble."

The spirit of religion is defeated, through the renewing of our mind Rom 12:2. Are we ready to move triumphantly into our new times, our new seasons, and our new destinies

Chapter 6
Breaking Off A Religious Spirit 2

Python Spirit

I believe that this spirit is at work in the church today, suffocating the life and fire of God out of people like a blanket and quenching the Holy Spirit in our lives and churches.

Now it happened, as we went to prayer, that a certain slave girl possessed with a spirit of divination met us, who brought her masters much profit by fortune-telling. This girl followed Paul and us, and cried out, saying, "These men are the servants of the Most High God, who proclaim to us the way of salvation." And this she did for many days. But Paul, greatly annoyed, turned and said to the spirit, "I command you in the name of Jesus Christ to come out of her." And he came out that very hour. But when her masters saw that their hope of profit was gone, they seized Paul and Silas and dragged them into the marketplace to the authorities. (Acts 16:16-19 NKJV)

In this passage of scripture, the spirit of divination is literally translated spirit of python in the Greek.

Divination, the art of obtaining secret knowledge, especially of the future, is a pagan counterpart of prophecy.

Some pythons have been reported to be 30 feet or more and 200 - 250 in pounds.

Killing of the prey happens by constriction and suffocation. When a python has you in its grips, each time you breath the grip tightens with each breath. Some have said the death process is slow, and when a python has you in its grip the only way to kill it is by cutting off its head.

When the python attacks, one or more coils of its body are thrown around the victim, and the powerful body muscles apply pressure. The pressure exerted by a large python must be terrific. The prey is killed, however, by suffocation rather than by any actual crushing of the ribs.

How A Python Attacks

This spirit wants to keep you from doing what God wants you to do. This is achieved best by the strategy of spiritual apathy. Python wants to quench through suffocation the life and breath of God from your lungs and crush your hopes, faith, visions, and dreams.

If the devil can crush your hopes, faith, visions and dreams than you will not have the fire you need to "press on to the mark of the high calling of God in Christ Jesus." The devil wants to get your drive, motivation, and fight. This is achieved in many ways. One in which the devil will whisper in your ears lies, accusations, condemnation, fear, and unbelief.

Psalm 74:14, talks about cutting the heads of the sea serpents and feeding it to the people in the wilderness. I believe that if we don't cut off the head, the speech center of python, then we to will come under the spirit of apathy and despair, closely linked to depression and the spirit of heaviness. The devil always attacks us with words like in the Garden of Eden in Genesis 3 the great question. "Has God indeed said?" The devil is always casting doubt and suspicion on God's word, and if we listen long enough, we to will be deceived of our inheritance lose heart and give up.

The Spirit Of Heaviness

To console those who mourn in Zion, To give them beauty for ashes, The oil of joy for mourning, The garment of praise for the spirit of heaviness; That they may be called trees of righteousness, the planting of the Lord, that He may be glorified. (Isaiah 61:3 NKJV)

The spirit of heaviness brings a spiritual cap in the spirit realm so God's people can only climb so high in the spirit. They have a low ceiling and low or no expectations. It can manifest with a sluggish weight during worship and weighs heavy on the countenance of the people in the meetings.

Python attacks in this way, squeezing the life, breath, and joy of the Lord from our lives.

One of the devil's number one attacks is hopelessness, despair, discouragement, and depression; it weighs us down and makes us tired.

40

Crushing and squeezing the life of God, faith, vision and hope out of the prophetic promises given to us from the Lord.

In the hearts of many of God's people is discouragement and spiritual apathy because hope deferred has made the heartsick and a sense of defeat and impossibility has set in concerning, taking the land.

We Are Well Able

In Numbers 13 when the 12 spies were sent in to spy out the land of promise, they returned with a bad report because of the giants in the land.

And they brought up an evil report of the land which they had searched unto the children of Israel, saying, The land, through which we have gone to search it, is a land that eateth up the inhabitants thereof; and all the people that we saw in it are men of a great stature. (Numbers 13:32 NKJV)

And they ascended by the south, and came unto Hebron; where Ahiman, Sheshai, and Talmai, the children of Anak, were. Their hearts had melted at the giants of Anak in the land. (Numbers 13:22 NKJV)

And they said;

Nevertheless, the people be strong that dwell in the land, and the cities are walled, and very great: and moreover, we saw the children of Anak there. (Numbers 13:28 NKJV)

They also said

And there we saw the giants, the sons of Anak, which come of the giants: and we were in our own sight as grasshoppers, and so we were in their sight. (Numbers 13:33 NKJV)

Even though God had promised it, they were not willing.

Send thou men, that they may search the land of Canaan, which I give unto the children of Israel. (Numbers 13:2 NKJV)

It was a done deal! God promised, but because of their perspective of the situation and the way it looked in the natural. Fear and discouragements gripped their heart and they got into unbelief at God's promise and did not enter the prophetic promise. Just like us today, we have several prophetic promises, dreams and hopes and we fail to enter because of discouragement and our perspective of our circumstances.

This is the way the spirit of python crushes our faith, vision, hope and dreams.

Through discouragements he causes depression, a sense of hopelessness and despair. Depression and the spirit of heaviness brings infirmity, defeat, and sickness.

If people can't see what God is doing, they stumble all over themselves; But when they attend to what he reveals, they are most blessed. (Proverbs 29:18 MESSAGE)

Spiritual Apathy Is Having No Fight Or Drive To Possess The Promises Of God.

Remember that the strategy of the spirit of python is to crush and suffocate the fire and life of God, using constriction and squeezing hope out of our hearts. Python wants to choke out the promise through strangling, using the power of hopelessness and discouragement.

The Hebrew translation of the word Anak for the giants in the land is: To choke as with strangulation using a necklace.

There are some that come to such a place in warfare associated with this spirit, and its slow death process, and constant feeling of weighing down. They want to commit suicide to end the pain.

Death and life are in the power of the tongue. (Proverbs 18:21 NASB)

One of the greatest hindrances to Christianity is religion. People get stuck in tradition, church doctrine and legalism, causing them to become unteachable. Satan then uses these people with a religious spirit to try and choke the life out of the Church.

This spirit must be defeated, its head must be cut off, and victory must be declared!

Recognize it. Do not pet it. Do not feed it. Do not let it grow. Kill it!

What Must We Do

Now that we know what the spirit of religion looks like and how it behaves, an important question remains: What are we to do about this?

The spirit of religion is one of the most diabolical forces opposing the Body of Christ. It is bold, intimidating, and ruthless. When it is present, it calls for courageous leaders to step forward.

The difficult nature of this spirit is that it hates to be revealed.

The people that are under its influence will go to great lengths to avoid any outward wrongdoing or weakness of character.

When confronted, they attempt to make the confronters feel judgmental and divisive.

If we allow room for this spirit to operate and fail to confront it, we will be in for a terrible time. As hard as it might be to deal with the spirit of religion, it must be done, or we will face heartache down the road.

The Priority Of Prayer

The first order of business is prayer. In the same manner that rain eventually softens dry hardened dirt, so intense intercession will soften the hardened resistance of those who are in bondage to the religious spirit, to confront the spirit.

The religious spirit will cause relationships to decay and will eventually bring about factions and division.

The Three-Step Process Toward Freedom

However, let us assume that a fruitful confrontation has taken place, humility prevails, and those who recognize the influence of the religious spirit in them desire deliverance. What then is the process?

All deliverance, including deliverance from the spirit of religion, requires three steps, which may be summed up in three words:

Repent

Renounce

Break

When dealing with the religious spirit, the repentance step will frequently involve repenting in areas of unforgiveness and participation in occult activity.

Often before coming to Christ, people are involved in the occult; and even uninformed believers may dabble in astrology, Ouija boards or other activity associated with the occult.

Generational iniquity often needs to be repented of, renounced, and broken as well.

This includes those in their family line who gave in to the religious spirit. Because of their failure to repent and remove the legal ground that they gave to the spirit, that spirit tends to seek a victim within the same family bloodline with which to partner.

Some people go by themselves to God with sincere and humble hearts and receive deliverance. Others submit themselves to church leadership and walk through the process of deliverance with them.

When I pastored, we had Encounter Weekends that dealt with these issues.

Steps To Repentance And Renouncing The Spirit Of Religion

At this time, I want you to take as long as you need to go through this, mean it with all your heart, speak it out loud because there is power in the tongue.

Generational:

I repent and renounce every opening, known or unknown that I have given to a religious spirit in my family line.

Personal Entry Points:

I repent and renounce every opening, known and unknown that I have given to a religious spirit and every work or darkness connected with it.

Point 1:

- I repent for not fully receiving Your love, compassion, mercy, grace, and forgiveness; and I renounce any belief that You, Lord are distant and judgmental. I choose to embrace all aspects of Your character and to intimately know You.

Point 2:

- I repent for allowing myself to be led by any other spirit than the Holy Spirit.
- I repent for relying on my own intellect in worship, praise, prayer, reading of the Word and spiritual warfare.
- I repent and renounce all legalism, traditions, and religious formulas.
- I repent and renounce all participation in dead works.
- I repent and renounce all dullness to the things of God.
- I repent and renounce hardness of heart.
- I choose for the oil of Your Holy Spirit to flow across my heart.

Point 3:

- I repent and renounce placing man's opinion of me above Yours.
- I repent and renounce compromises: of the truth, of my integrity and of my purity.
- I repent and renounce all compromises in my attitude toward sin.
- I repent for my lack of transparency:
    o For covering sin.
    o For not confessing sin.
    o For not receiving correction.
    o For being defensive and quick to justify and rationalize my sin.
- I repent and renounce all deception and hypocrisy.
- I repent and renounce all pride, arrogance, and self-righteousness.
- I repent and renounce all comparison, judgment, criticism, gossip, jealousy, covetousness, and anger.

- I repent and renounce every act of rebellion that has reinforced the spirit of religion in my life.
- I choose to have obedience as my heart attitude.
- I choose to no longer partner with the same spirit that killed Jesus and that continues to attempt to kill the work of the Holy Spirit today.
- I choose to no longer oppose God.

Break

I break every hex, curse or vow, every spell, incantation, or ritual.

I break every covenant and blood covenant, every sacrifice and blood sacrifice.

I break every soul tie, every generational tie in my family line.

I break any other legal right known or unknown, for the spirit of religion to stay.

Spirit of religion, as the Body of Christ, I and those with me come against you:

We refuse to allow you to steal our intimate relationship with our Lord.

We refuse to allow you to kill the flow of the Holy Spirit in us.

We refuse to allow you to destroy the anointing of others through us.

We choose to receive the anointing to break the power of the spirit of religion in the Church of Jesus Christ.

With all sincerity, humility, and submission to Christ I have gone through this list of statements and declarations. I am now assured that the religious spirit, no matter how deeply it has been imbedded, has left. I am now free to move powerfully into the destiny that God has for me, individually and corporately.

Chapter 7
Kingdom of God 1

Kingdom Principles

These principles are so powerful, they changed my life, how I thought about myself, about God and others. These principles changed my behavior in how I treated others and how I ministered. I want to encourage you to take your time reading and studying and let these principles get embedded in your spirit as to transform your life.

Kingdom believers are no longer under the law; they are now accountable to the Spirit of Christ to examine their own hearts according to their obedience to the Word of God and His small still voice. The Kingdom of Righteousness allows us to be more like Christ.

Just something to think about. Luke 2:25 Simeon (Law) was in the Temple waiting for the messiah to be dedicated, he had been told by the Holy Spirit that he would not die until he had seen the Lord's Christ's. Vs. 29 he (law) departed in peace. Vs. 36-38 Anna (Grace) arrives in after Simeon (law) left.

Fatherhood of God- Followers of Judaism knew of the God of the Old Testament by his attributes as exhibited by the various names of God proclaimed through the experiences of the patriarchs and Old Testament saints. They were aware of the all-powerful God of Moses, the great I AM, who delivered the Children of Israel from bondage in Egypt. And they knew the God of Abraham who provided a ram in the bush for a sacrifice in place of Abraham's only son Isaac.

In contrast to the names traditionally used to describe or address God (Yahweh, Elohim, Adonai), Jesus chose a different and more intimate expression – the Aramaic term Abba ('Father') By addressing God in this manner, Jesus showed that the same God who had all the prior Old Testament attributes of power, omnipresence, and omniscience, now is a God who is capable of being known intimately and personally.

In the Gospel of John, Jesus frequently addressed his relationship with the Father in this way. He talked about how the Father had shown him, all the things the Father had done (John 5:20). He talked about being sent by the Father to accomplish a task (John 6:39). These references indicate a Father who is involved in the life and affairs of his children, and within reach, available.

Family – priesthood of believers - The arrival of the Kingdom of God through the life and ministry of Jesus also initiated the concept of the family of God in a new way.

Judaism had begun with the 12 tribes of Israel and their God with his laws. But it was only the Levites who were chosen to approach God on behalf of the other tribes. With the onset of the Kingdom of God, as Jesus taught his disciples to pray the Lord's Prayer, it was understood by the early believers to be a prayer, specifically identifying them as Kingdom people, those in the family of God.

More specifically, the Kingdom initiated the priesthood of all believers, who, based on right standing and reconciliation, could go boldly into the throne of God, who was now their personal heavenly Father.

Realized power was another principle of the Kingdom of God

It was not a kingdom characterized by lofty ideas and long prayers as with the religious leaders that were powerless to bring about change.

People were spiritually enlightened and blessed as their needs were met in extraordinary ways in the ministry of Jesus through his miracles, healings, and deliverance. As people were made whole, they were able to experience the power of God in ways they had never experienced prior to that time.

As Jesus ministered, he ushered in a new beginning, a kingdom of believers united as the family of a God with whom they could have intimacy, personal access, and involvement of God in the daily affairs of their lives.

Regardless of their social status in life, they could be included in this kingdom which was freely given to them. Jesus demonstrated the Kingdom of God with power and authority.

Some Of The People God Used

He chose a stuttering Moses to lead four million Israelites out of bondage to Egypt, with only a rod.

He chose young David to kill the giant Goliath with only a slingshot.

God used Gideon's army of only two hundred to defeat thousands. Nothing is impossible with God. We only need to make ourselves available to Him

So, Jesus said to them again, "Peace to you! As the Father has sent Me, I also send you." (John 20:21 NKJV)

"And as you go, preach, saying, 'The kingdom of heaven is at hand.' "Heal the sick, cleanse the lepers, raise the dead, cast out demons. Freely you have received, freely give. (Matthew 10:7, 8 NKJV)

Because He is alive in you, everything you do (Kingdom business, service, product or ministry), is a platform from which you have been given to exalt your Heavenly Father and to manifest the Kingdom of God!

This is the essence of walking in "the sweet spot", in the divine design of your assignment, your destiny!

"And this gospel of the kingdom will be preached in all the world as a witness to all the nations, and then the end will come. (Matthew 24:14 NKJV)

"But I will come—and soon—if the Lord lets me, and then I'll find out whether these arrogant people just give pretentious speeches or whether they really have God's power. For the Kingdom of God is not just a lot of talk; it is living by God's power." (1 Corinthians 4:19, 20 NLT)

Prove It

And do not be conformed to this world, but be transformed by the renewing of your mind, so that you may prove what the will of God is, that which is good and acceptable and perfect. (Rom 12:2 NASB) What is the will of God on this earth, do we know it and are we willing to declare and demonstrate on this earth? Thy Kingdom come; thy will be done on earth as it is in heaven.

The central message of Jesus Christ was the message of "the Kingdom of God" or "the Kingdom of Heaven". This message, when understood, is the most relevant message for the needs of humanity. It is a highly attractive message and will produce the greatest results of any message one could give. This message must once again become the central theme of preachers and teachers in these last days.

When the message of the Kingdom of God is given correctly, the results will be dramatic, just as they were for our Lord and for the apostles of our Lord. For with the proclamation of the Kingdom comes the demonstration (power) of the Kingdom. Paul declared in 1 Corinthians 4:20 "for the Kingdom of God is not in word but in power". Anyone who attempts to preach or teach about the Kingdom of God without demonstrating something of the reality the power of the Kingdom has missed the mark.

John The Baptist Preached The Message Of The Kingdom

"In those days John the Baptist came preaching in the wilderness of Judea, and saying, "Repent, for the kingdom of heaven is at hand." (Matthew 3:1,2 NASB)

Jesus Preached The Message Of The Kingdom

From that time Jesus began to preach and to say, "Repent, for the kingdom of heaven is at hand." (Matthew 4:17 NASB)

"And Jesus went about all Galilee, teaching in their synagogues, preaching the gospel of the kingdom, and healing all kinds of sicknesses and all kinds of diseases among the people. Then His fame went throughout all Syria; and they brought to Him all sick people who were afflicted with various diseases and torments, and those who were demon-possessed, epileptics, and paralytics; and He healed them." (Matthew 4:23, 24 NKJV)

Many other references could be given from the gospels demonstrating that this was in fact the principal message of Jesus Christ. Many of Jesus' parables were about the Kingdom. He gave the secrets of the Kingdom to his apostles.

50

Paul Preached The Message Of The Kingdom

"And indeed, now I know that you all, among whom I have gone preaching the kingdom of God, will see my face no more." (Acts 20:25 NKJV)

Jesus Called Men/Us To Preach The Message Of The Kingdom

"Jesus said to him, 'Let the dead bury their own dead, but you go and preach the kingdom of God.'" (Luke 9:60 NIV)

Jesus Predicted the Continued Preaching of 'This Gospel of the Kingdom' until His Second Coming

"And this gospel of the Kingdom will be preached in all the world as a witness to all the nations, and then the end will come." (Matthew 24:14 NKJV)

Not only do we have Jesus and Paul as examples in this matter of preaching the Kingdom. We have the assurance from Jesus' own lips that this message of the kingdom should be preached 'as a witness' or 'with demonstration' to all the world. This is the main task of the church.

What Is The Message Of The Kingdom

Some view the Kingdom of God as an alternative term for "heaven", but Jesus taught that it could be in our midst on earth, and come to us now through His ministry - for example - the ministry of casting out demons by the Spirit of God, then the Kingdom of God has come upon me. (Matthew 12:28).

When Jesus spoke of entering the Kingdom he was not merely saying "going to heaven when you die". He was talking about entering the Kingdom life here and now. This includes heaven later, and whatever plans God may have for us on the new earth, but it is far more than that. The Kingdom of Heaven is not about "sitting on the clouds singing holy, holy, holy for eternity".

The Kingdom of God is the place where Jesus is King, and we are heirs of His Kingdom. It is a spiritual, invisible kingdom which has made its presence felt in the affairs of this earth. It is not confined to a particular geographical location, nor to a particular religious organization.

The Kingdom is truly present in a place to the extent that Christ is honored as King and He has rule reign dominion and authority over our lives. Kingdom - Government

There is an opposing kingdom at work. Jesus spoke of Satan's kingdom (Matthew 12:26). The Scripture declares that "the whole world lies under the sway of the evil one" (1 John 5:19). Satan is called "the god of this age" (2 Corinthians 4:4), "the prince of the power of the air" and "the spirit who now works in the sons of disobedience"

(Ephesians 2:2). Satan, operating through a vast hierarchical network of fallen angels, evil spirits, or demons as they are variously known, exercises a stupendous influence on the hearts and lives of men, women, boys, and girls. The existence of Satan's kingdom accounts for the hatred, the wars, the stupidity and selfishness of mankind, the existence of false religions and philosophies and the presence of every kind of perversion and deception on the face of the earth.

Satanic influence is highly effective because it operates in the background and is generally not openly displayed. It is almost always covered under another name or philosophy.

The kingdom of God is in perpetual conflict with the spiritual kingdom of Satan. These are the two spiritual kingdoms which dominate the affairs of mankind and influence the lives of multitudes. They are totally opposite in nature. There is no third kingdom. The kingdom of God only advances through the destruction of the works and influence of the devil.

Three Ways To Come Against The Enemy

1. You displace powers and principalities by bringing light into darkness. Jesus is the light!
2. You tear down strongholds – house of thoughts, wrong thinking, stinking thinking you establish a righteousness stronghold.
3. You cast out demons

James 4:7 If we submit to God and resist the devil.

52

What Are The Results Of The Kingdom

Paul said, "The kingdom of God is not eating and drinking, but righteousness, peace and joy in the Holy Spirit." (Romans 14:17). God's kingdom in someone's heart will rightly position them before God, and the peace and joy of God will be their state of being. Out of our position comes peace and joy. If you have lost your peace or joy you do not have to look far. Somehow you got out of position, something is wrong with your relationship with the Lord.

If people only understood and believed this, then they would make every effort to welcome the Kingdom of God/ Govt of God into their lives, allowing Him to have rule, reign, dominion, and authority. This applies to Christians as well as unbelievers.

When Philip the evangelist preached Christ in Samaria, "there was great joy in the city" (Acts 8:8). Today we need such a manifestation of the Kingdom of God in our cities.

The message of the Kingdom of God applies not only at the individual level, but also at the corporate level.

The key is faith that recognizes and values the works of Jesus Christ and His presence above all else. Faith that values the Word of God and that small still voice (Holy Spirit) above all other authorities, influences or suggestions.

The result in every community is the practice of justice, mercy, love, faithfulness, favor, and blessing, the things that people in the world long for.

Because the church has largely failed to demonstrate and to preach these things of the Kingdom people have been willing to look for them in other directions.

Divine Healing Is A Sign Of The Kingdom

When God made Adam and Eve, no sickness was present. Sickness is a breakdown in the created order. When the body is no longer in divine order, sickness is the result. However, when the Kingdom of God manifests in a person's body, divine healing and health is the result. Every divine healing done through the power of the Holy Spirit is a manifestation of the

53

Kingdom of God.

And He gave some as apostles, and some as prophets, some as evangelists, some as pastors and teachers, for the equipping of the saints for the work of ministry, for the building up of the body of Christ. (Ephesians 4:11 NASB) That word equip means alignment like putting a broken bone together. When you reset and align the bone it heals and causes you to function properly. It brings proper order, original order. When order and alignment happen, it brings healing.

Some denominations read Eph. 4:11 like this; And He gave ... some evangelists, some pastors and teachers. This comes totally against everything you were taught in Hermeneutics, properly interpreting the Word of God.

It is a matter of record that many, if not most, of the healings done by Jesus were done for those who were oppressed by the devil (Acts 10:38). Most sickness is caused by demons - either directly or indirectly. Because large portions of the church have been ineffective in dealing with demons, there has been a corresponding ineffectiveness in dealing with sickness in the name of Jesus.

Sickness represents the kingdom of Satan in a person's body. When sickness is driven out in the name of Jesus, the Kingdom of God advances. These healings are done by the power of the Holy Spirit. The Holy Spirit moves in with his power when we really believe and operate in faith. This faith is the gift of God - it comes through the recognition of Jesus, the reality of God's Kingdom, and through personal relationship with the Godhead.

Since physical healing is something that people can see in the natural realm, it is therefore also a sign of the Kingdom of God. It is a biblical tool for evangelism. Divine healing accompanied Jesus constantly as he preached and taught about the Kingdom. This was not only to authenticate He is the Messiah (Matthew 11:4-6), but also as a demonstration of the truth of the message of the Kingdom of God.

Divine healings were also done because of the Lord's compassion (Matthew 8:1-4), and His desire to destroy the works of the devil (1 John 3:8) and to do the will of God in all things. All this relates to the message of the Kingdom of God.

What Is The Fruit Of the Kingdom

If the Kingdom of God means God's effective rulership in things, His rule, reign, dominion, and authority, then what is the fruit of the Kingdom? The fruit of God's Kingdom includes every blessing man can enjoy. Salvations, miracles, signs, wonders, deliverance, and empowerment. That is basically the Kingdom of God being manifested on this earth.

True justice in human affairs, love in human relationships, the absence of tormenting fear, as well as the manifestation of all the fruit of the Holy Spirit mentioned in Galatians 5:22-23 are just some of the fruits.

Spiritual revival is the result of a large-scale penetration of the Kingdom message and power in a society.

In addition to these spiritual and social blessings, the penetration of God's Kingdom will bring prosperity and success in natural affairs.

The Devil Will

- **Take You Further Than You Want To Go**
- **Keep You Longer Than You Want To Stay**
- **Charge You More Than You Want To Pay**

Sin is extremely expensive to any people or nation. Just the use of drugs alone costs America more than 100 billion dollars per year.

The cost of laziness, dishonesty in any society is beyond the power of any man to calculate in dollar terms. The penetration of the message of the kingdom progressively removes these factors.

To the extent that the Kingdom manifests, people begin to work in harmony with respect for one for another. No one cheats or steals or behaves foolishly. More people apply kingdom principles such as diligence, perseverance, faith, and vision, resulting in greater prosperity and success.

All this is fine if people remain thankful towards God and dependent upon God. The temptation to renounce the effective Lordship of the King and get into pride when all seems to be going well is well known in the history both of Israel and of many Christian nations. It always has serious consequences in the end. We are called to seek God when things are going

55

well, as well as in times of trial.

God wants to bless families, individuals, churches, and nations. Satan seeks to weaken all the above, so that he can enslave, destroy, mock and torment. The good news is that God has not left us helpless against Satan and his powers. We have the Word of God himself, the power of His Spirit, and the authority of the name of Jesus. However, all of these must be understood, received, and applied in our daily lives for us to reap the benefits.

We come into this, by coming into alignment with the Spirit of Christ Rom 8:9, the government of God, His rule, reign, dominion, and authority in our own lives. Self-government, allowing the government of God, have rule, reign, dominion, and authority in our mind, will, and emotions; how we think about things, make decisions and how we feel about things, that is Kingdom living.

If we come into alignment with our assignment, with what God has called us to do; we will have rule, reign, dominion, and authority. We are called to declare, demonstrate, and establish the Kingdom of God.

And do not be conformed to this world, but be transformed by the renewing of your mind, so that you may prove what the will of God is, that which is good and acceptable and perfect. (Romans 12:2 NASB)

The Kingdom Of God Advances

The gospels reveal that Jesus spent much time casting out demons. Some foolish theologians feel this is basically irrelevant to Christian ministry today, but in doing so, they reveal their spiritual ignorance. In the matter of casting out demons, God has hidden these things from the wise and learned but revealed them to babes (Luke 10:17-21).

The things of the Kingdom are often missed by theologians with doctorate degrees, while "unschooled and ignorant" men, women, and even children not only know them, but also effectively apply them. Jesus said to his disciples who wanted to know who is greatest in the Kingdom of Heaven, that unless they became as little children, they would not even enter the Kingdom of Heaven. This is a relevant word for many present-day leaders of Christian denominations to whom the significance of this ministry of deliverance is hidden, just as Jesus said it would be from the "wise and

56

prudent". They may have elaborate theological arguments to defend their positions of spiritual powerlessness. However, on the day of judgment we will see whose word will stand - theirs or the Lords.

The Kingdom belongs to the "poor in spirit" (Matthew 5:3). There is the poor that has no material things. There is the poor in spirit, Lord I can do nothing without you, I am totally dependent on you Lord for everything.

The reality is that the church has been subjected to a demonic invasion which has robbed it of most of the blessings of the Kingdom. Over the years certain denominations have preached against the worldly things, bowling, movies, and roller skating or we are against this ministry or that ministry, teaching and preaching more on what we are against than what we are for.

We are called to equip the saints, empower them, and help them to discover their identity, purpose and destiny, teaching them the Kingdom of God and how to move with authority, healing the sick, casting out demons and setting the captives free.

The Kingdom of God is not the same as the Church. Many of the churches are where Satan has a large measure of effective control. This is evidenced not only by false doctrine, but also by a lack of love and the presence of all kinds of relational and personal sin.

The Kingdom of God message tells us to bow the knee to Jesus and get the sin out of our lives. The presence of sickness in so many Christians is again evidence that the message of the Kingdom of God concerning divine healing has not been preached and demonstrated as it ought to be. Sin has opened the door to demonic oppression, and unbelief has held the church in bondage. The lack of true anointing in many churches is another proof that the church and the Kingdom are not the same."

When I broke free of the religious mindset and began to fully embrace the Kingdom of God, the principles, the mindset and the culture it changed my life.

Chapter 8
Kingdom of God 2

Meaning of the term Kingdom, the primary meaning of malkuth (Hebrew) and basileia (Greek) is the authority, reign, or rule of a king. The territory, subjects, and operations of the kingdom are secondary meanings.

When Jesus speaks of being in and living in the Kingdom, we are talking about obedience to His rule, reign, dominion, and authority in our lives. Jesus is the King of kings and Lord of lords.

The Kingdom Of God - The Sphere Of God's Rule

For the Kingdom is the Lord's and He rules over the nations. (Psalm 22:28 NASB)

Though rightfully under God's rule, fallen human beings nonetheless participate in universal rebellion against God and His authority. We know that we are of God, and that the whole world lies in the power of the evil one. Vs 20 And we know that the Son of God has come and has given us understanding so that we may know Him who is true; and we are in Him who is true, in His Son Jesus Christ. This is the true God and eternal life. (1 John 5:19,20 NASB) We give You thanks, Lord God, the Almighty, the One who is and was, because You have taken great power and have begun to reign. (Revelation 11:17 NASB)

However, by faith and obedience men and women turn from their rebellion, are regenerated by the Holy Spirit, and become a part of the Kingdom and its operation. While participation in the kingdom of God is not compulsory, the Kingdom is present, whether people recognize and accept it or not.

The kingdom of God is both a present reality now and a promise of future fulfillment.

The Kingdom was present on earth in the person and acts of Jesus during the time of His Incarnation. After the Resurrection, the Risen Christ is present by His Spirit, and where His Spirit is, the Kingdom is present. The Kingdom is manifested in the church we are the church.

Plants- one dimension –body

Animals – two dimensional – body – mind

Humans – three dimensional – spirit-soul- body. When Adam & Eve sinned, the spirit went offline. When we are born again, the spirit of Christ, the Holy Spirit comes and lives within, the Spirit is back online.

Illus: Circuit breaker pops and the lights go out, and now we must keep the resistance out.

"The Kingdom of God is within: Strong's Number 1787 [entos, "within," "in the midst," or "among"] you" nor will they say, 'Look here it is!' or, 'There it is!' For behold, the Kingdom of God is in your midst." (Luke 17:21 NASB)

Old things have passed away, all things become new. We can see different; we can hear different and walk different. It is all about obedience and submission to God's word and the Holy Spirit.

The restored reign of God has become a reality. By Jesus accomplishing redemption through His death, burial, and resurrection He is reclaiming the usurped territory on earth through us the church.

There are forceful spiritual confrontations between the power of the Kingdom of God and the powers that dominate the world in this present age.

The Holy Spirit - The Kingdom Of God

The four Gospels mention the Kingdom 86 times. Jesus spoke more about the Kingdom than any other subject.

"Your kingdom come" (Matthew 6:10). The Kingdom is already among us in that it has invaded Satan's domain and has assured final victory. The Kingdom comes in a measure whenever a person receives Christ as Savior, is healed, or delivered, or is touched in any way by the divine.

God choses to rule and reign through us. As we understand God's word to a greater extent and cultivate an intimate relationship with the Holy Spirt we will experience a greater measure of His manifest presence (glory), we will be able to see more of what is happening in the spiritual realm.

We see through the lens of God's word. Faith comes by hearing and hearing by the word of God.

Spiritual Realm Vs Physical Realm

Our Father is a good father and a good God. He is not out to hurt or harm us in any way. He never plans for evil, but He always plans to bring good out of every situation we face. When we start to trust in Him and what He wants to show us about things happening in our lives and bodies, we can start to see how deeply that goodness can flow. We must not be the ones who determine the outcome, but who instead submit the outcome to Him, trusting in His processes.

And we know that God causes all things to work together for good to those who love God, to those who are called according to His purpose. (Romans 8:28 NASB)

To live with one's eyes closed to this spiritual reality, to go through life thinking that the physical and material world is all there is, is a path that leads to emptiness. Utter emptiness. Material things alone cannot satisfy the longing within the human heart.

There is a deep hunger for something more, for contact with another dimension of reality, for interaction with the spiritual realm, for connection and communication with God.

Faith Is Not Blind

We walk by faith, not by sight. (2 Corinthians 5:7 NASB) Faith in God's word and the death, burial, and resurrection of Jesus Christ. I hear many talking about blind faith, but real faith is not blind. Real faith is when we trust in what we see by the spirit. The Bible says to walk by faith and not by sight, but this does not mean that faith is blind. It means that faith is not limited to physical sight.

There are many scriptures that talk about spiritual sight. We will read just a few.

Truly, truly, I say to you, unless someone is born again, he cannot see the kingdom of God." (John 3:3 NASB)

If we cannot see God, it is because we are not looking. He is the rewarder of those who diligently seek Him. (Heb 11:6) But from there you will seek the Lord your God, and you will find Him if you search for Him with all your heart and all your soul. (Deut. 4:29 NASB)

We will only see whatever it is that we are looking for.

Look

To direct your eyes for the purpose of seeing something

To observe with the eyes while keeping them directed

To seek, to search

To expect

The Natural Eye

The lens sits behind the iris and is clear and colorless. The lens job is to focus light rays on the back of the eyeball – a part called the retina. The retina takes the light the eye receives and changes it into nerve signals so the brain can understand what the eye is seeing.

The spirit of a person is the lamp of the Lord, searching all the innermost parts of his being. (Proverbs 20:27 NASB) We realize as the eye is to the body, the spirit of man is to his soul. Just as your eye perceives material things, your spirit perceives spiritual truths. Spiritual perception.

The Importance Of Spiritual Sight

It is possible for our spiritual sight to grow dim. We could even become blind. Unlike natural blindness, which is obvious to all, the spiritually blind are often deceived and think they see. The people of Laodicea could not see their true condition. They thought they were rich and in need of nothing which was the exact opposite of the truth. (Rev 3:17-19 NASB)

My people perish for lack of vision. Message version: If people cannot see what God is doing, they stumble all over themselves; But when they attend to what he reveals, they are most blessed. (Proverbs 29:18 MESSAGE)

They cast off restraint. Backsliding always starts with a lack of spiritual sight. Revelation begins to grow dim. When the vision fades, the feeling fades, the passion fades, the fire goes out.

Spiritual sight is vital to effective ministry. Jesus said that He only did what he saw the Father doing. (John 5:19-20 NIV)

How Can We See Spiritually

Anoint your eyes with eye salve (Cultivate the presence of the Lord through worship, prayer, obedience. (Rev 3:18 KJV) Position ourselves to see. Stop looking at the wrong things and start looking at the right things. (Phil 4:8 NASB)

Spend Time in the Light

In the natural realm, it does not do you any good to have your eyes open if you are in a pitch-black room. Without light, there is nothing to see. The same goes for the spiritual realm. It would not do you any good to have your eyes open if you were living in darkness.

Where Does Spiritual Light Come from

This is the message we have heard from him and declare to you: God is light; in him there is no darkness at all. (1 John 1:5 NIV)

And how do we enter that light?

Jesus said, "I have come into the world as a light, so that no one who believes in me should stay in darkness." (John 12:46 NIV)

Ask The Lord To Open Your Eyes

When it comes to spiritual eyes, our usual problem is not that our eyes are simply closed, but rather we are blind.

God the Father sent Jesus to open eyes that are blind, to free captives from prison and to release from the dungeon those who sit in darkness. (Isaiah 42:7 NIV)

Jesus said, "I know your deeds, that you are neither cold nor hot. I wish you were either one or the other! So, because you are lukewarm— neither hot nor cold—I am about to spit you out of my mouth. You say, 'I am rich; I have acquired wealth and do not need a thing.' But you do not realize that you are wretched, pitiful, poor, blind, and naked. I counsel you to buy from me gold refined in the fire, so you can become rich; and white clothes to wear, so you can cover your shameful nakedness; and salve to put on your eyes, so you can see. Those whom I love I rebuke and discipline. So be earnest and repent." (Revelation 3:15-19 NIV)

Exercise Your Spiritual Senses

When Jesus opened the apostle Paul's spiritual eyes, He gave him a mission:

I am sending you to them to open their eyes and turn them from darkness to light, and from the power of Satan to God, so that they may receive forgiveness of sins and a place among those who are sanctified by faith in me. (Acts 26:17b-18 NIV)

If you are walking in the light, then you need to invite others into that light. Proclaim the Good News of Jesus Christ through the power of the Holy Spirit. Continue to exercise your spiritual eyes. Engage in the hope to which you have been called in Christ. Perceive the spiritual realm. Discover revelation in the Word of God. Recognize the presence of Jesus in everyday circumstances. See opportunities for evangelism. And keep the focus of your life on Jesus Christ.

I pray that the eyes of your heart may be enlightened, so that you will know what is the hope of His calling, what are the riches of the glory of His inheritance in the saints, and what is the boundless greatness of His power toward us who believe. (Ephesians 1:18-19a NASB)

For us to understand the Kingdom, see what God is doing on this earth and fulfill our Kingdom mandate, we must have our spiritual eyes and ears opened continually.

Chapter 9
Receiving Healing

Medicine And Doctors

THERE is absolutely nothing wrong with using conventional medicine if you are a Christian. It is neither evil nor lack of faith in God to do so. I think it is important to appreciate that God, in his infinite wisdom, created certain plants with medicinal properties so you will discover that almost all medicines are made from plants. He also found it fitting to impart to man wisdom and knowledge about the human body and how it functions.

Besides conventional medicines, however, God has given us another, all-powerful healing medicine in the form of His word.

"My son attend to my words; incline thine ear unto my sayings. Let them not depart from thine eyes; keep them in the midst of thine heart. For they are life unto those that find them, and health to all their flesh." (Proverbs 4:20-22 KJV)

He sent His word and healed them and delivered them from their destructions. (Psalm 107:20 KJV)

If we are to receive from God, there are some things we need to believe and do.

Believe And Know God Loves You And God Desires To Heal You

Our foundation scripture for this is (John 3:16 KJV) For God so loved the world, that He gave His only begotten Son, that whosoever believeth in Him should not perish, but have everlasting life. He loved us before we ever knew Him, He accepts us with all our baggage.

The very nature of God is love. Whoever does not love does not know God, because God is love. (1 John 4:8 NIV)

Love is not something He chooses to do or give; it is the very essence of who He is. He does not just love, He is love. And so, we know and rely on the love God has for us. God is love. Whoever lives in love lives in God, and God in them. (John 4:16 NIV)

Love motivates His every action, directs His activities, and reflects His desires. This is love: not that we loved God, but that he loved us and sent his Son as an atoning for ours sins.   (1 John 4:10 NIV)

We live in a culture today, for the most part operates in conditional love, a love of convenience, "I will love you as long as you add value to my life and please me. When that ceases so does my love for you".

This attitude stands in stark contrast to God's unconditional love, which never fails.

But I am like an olive tree flourishing in the house of God; I trust God's unfailing love for ever and ever. (Psalm 52:8 NIV)

Praise the Lord. Give thanks to the Lord, for he is good; his love endures forever. (Psalm 106:1 NIV)

God's love is not motivated by personal gain. Unconditional love does not mean that God loves everything we do, but rather His love is so intense that he loves every sinner, no matter how vile and despicable he or she may be in the eyes of humanity, so much that he provides a way for them to find love, life and holiness.

"Intense love does not measure, it just gives" (Mother Teresa)

The Focus Of God's Love Is Redemption

God's unconditional love and intense love for fallen humanity motivated the plan of salvation. And from Jesus Christ, who is the faithful witness, the firstborn from the dead, and the ruler of the kings of the earth. To him who loves us and has freed us from our sins by his blood. (Rev. 1:5 NIV)

Simply, salvation is God making us whole or complete. It is a healing of the soul, bringing us back to the same state of Adam when God breathed life into him and made him a living soul.

When we look at God's love, we see the full picture of salvation, Sozo is the Greek word for salvation.

Sozo is the Greek word for salvation, yet its root meaning goes beyond just the forgiveness of sins. According to Strong's Concordance, Sozo also carries the idea of being physically healed of diseases and to be delivered from your enemy.

When we receive God's love, we receive his forgiveness, healing, freedom and much more.

The Goal Of God's Love Is Relationship

Love requires relationship, as love is a dynamic force or presence that naturally seeks expression. Simply put love loves! And to do that there must be an object of that love or it is incomplete.

Our relationship with God should be an intimate one. There is a sacred knowledge and expression that takes place in our relationship with the Lord. To know him intimately is to open the door for revelation and fulfillment. It brings change or transformation-change of essence, expression, behavior, desires, identity, and security.

When we come to a greater understanding of God's redemption and the value of an intimate relationship with him is when we walk in all of what he has redeemed that was lost through Adam in the Garden.

The most important thing to learn from this is we will not receive all the God has for us until we know God unconditionally loves us. This helps us to not only receive but is so important when ministering to others. We will tell ourselves or others will tell us, God do not love you. We know that is not true.

God Is A Giver

"But without faith it is impossible to please him; for he that cometh to God must believe that he is, and that he is a rewarder of them that diligently seek him." (Hebrews 11:6 KJV)

If we diligently seek him, he proves he is a rewarder. This is an important principle; we must seek him through his word and an intimate relationship.

When we come say, "Lord, I believe you are," and then say, "I believe if I seek you, You are a rewarder."

Christianity is not a passive religion. We are not called to simply sit and wait doing nothing for God to move, our responsibility is to continue to pursue and persevere daily trusting God for the power and strength to walk in His life and light.

I am convinced our healing, our miracle, our breakthrough is not where we are standing or sitting, it is where we are about to step. Faith is an action word, and we must be willing to take that step of faith if we are to see that thing manifested on earth.

"But seek ye first the kingdom of God and his righteousness; and all these things shall be added unto you." (Matthew 6:33 KJV)

Ask, and it shall be given to you; seek, and you shall find; knock, and it will be opened to you. For everyone who asks receives, and he who seeks finds, and to him who knocks it will be opened unto you. (Matthew 7:7 KJV)

We Must Forgive And Not Carry Offenses

Unforgiveness blocks God's blessings from flowing in your life. One of the greatest choices one can be faced with … forgive and forget or hold on and never let go.

People often feel that it is easier to simply shut others out who have hurt them, but in reality, this leads to a closed spirit, heartache, bitterness, and can even turn to physical pain and suffering in the long run.

God wants to bless you, heal your body, bring breakthrough, but a bitter unforgiving mindset will block you from receiving the very thing God wants you to have in life … freedom!

For if you forgive others for their transgressions, your heavenly Father will also forgive you. But if you do not forgive others, then your Father will not forgive your transgressions. (Matthew 6:14,15 NASB)

God makes it clear that for us to receive forgiveness we must be able to forgive others.

Is it worth it to miss out on heaven's blessings, miss out on our healing, our breakthrough just because of our refusal to forgive?

That kind of mindset will never hurt the person or circumstance that did us wrong, it will only hurt us!

Meditate On God's Word

To know God's will for our life we must know His word!

The Bible is the essential and primary source for knowing God and His will for our lives. The art of understanding and applying God's word is the Holy Spirit's primary means of transforming us into Christlikeness.

As we begin to meditate on God's word it is always important to thank and praise God for His revelation of Himself to us through His word and ask Him to help us build a solid foundation in His absolute truth.

I tell people to read and study God's word, but study for more than just information, study for experience, for application and for transformation.

We study to; know Jesus, we study to prepare ourselves for disciple-making, ministry and service, we study for personal transformation and we study to understand God's character and attributes, we need to keep this in mind when we get into the word of God so we can be intentional.

Be diligent to present yourself approved to God as a worker who does not need to be ashamed, accurately handling the word of truth. (2 Timothy 2:15 NASB)

The Greek word used to describe "accurately handle" in 2 Timothy 2:15 means "to cut straight" and was used to describe the clearing and leveling of a path or road. We are to study God's word in a correct and direct manner as if we are traveling a straight path, avoiding distracting and dangerous detours. This involves preparation, precision and focus as if we were doing the surgery.

Always personalize God's word when you are reading it.

One great way to do that is to put your name in the place of pronouns or nouns.

For example, John 3:16 For God so loved John he gave His only begotten Son so that John would not parish but have everlasting life.

Philippians 1:6 "For I am confident of this one thing, that He who began a good work in John will perfect it until the day of Christ Jesus.

Read the word like God is directly talking to you.

Reading God's word is about getting to know the author of the Word, getting to know Him personally!

When we begin to view God's Word as his love written personally to us to help us navigate this journey called life, we will not want to go a day without reading the Bible.

Every day is a new challenge and with each day I need wisdom, strategy and understanding to help me navigate throughout the day, to help me help others in bringing resolve. I am constantly seeking strategies and wisdom through His Word and through communicating with the Holy Spirit through my relationship with Him.

God's Word will never change your life until you let it become personal. The Bible becomes dynamic when it becomes specific.

There are so many struggling in their walk because they do not know what God's word says about them or their situation. Many live-in fear and depression because of this. It does not have to be this way.

Cultivate An Intimacy With The Holy Spirit

How can we grow in intimacy with the Holy Spirit?

We have all heard of individuals soaking, going into their prayer closets, getting away for a week or so with the Holy Spirit for a time of refreshing and hearing from the Holy Spirit. This is important and has great outcomes, but we know most are busy in their schedule with their job, family, and life.

Special times spent in God's Presence are vital to those of us who want to grow in our relationship with the Holy Spirit.

I love the times when I can spend extended times with the Word of God and the Holy Spirit, but I have found I have to be very intentional in setting those times aside.

I learned years ago how to pray without ceasing, how to recognize that the Holy Spirit is with me everywhere and I can call out to Him without going through religious mechanics.

I am not saying getting alone with God for extended periods is religious but I am saying we can bring a lot of extras into it thinking we have to do it this way to please God such as, a certain posture; bended knee, eyes closed or certain atmosphere, very quiet or certain worship music. It is amazing how the Holy Spirit can speak to us at a football game or a crowded mall.

The key is to learn how to pray without ceasing.

Be cheerful no matter what; pray all the time; thank God no matter what happens. This is the way God wants you who belong to Christ Jesus to live. (1 Thessalonians 5:16-18 MESSAGE)

I keep myself in an attitude of sensing His presence, hearing that still small voice, feeling that check or sense in my spirit that the Holy Spirit is wanting to get my attention. Many times, throughout the day I am praying out loud and sometimes under my breath when around a crowd and it helps me to stay sensitive to the Holy Spirit's presence.

Always walk with a grateful heart.

Be real, you do not have to get all King James' version in your prayers, just have a conversation with the Holy Spirit like you would with anyone else. Talk to Him about your day, the exciting things in your life. Talk to Him about your concerns involving you and concerns involving others. Just be real!

Talk to Him while you are working.

Talk to Him while you are waiting.

When you mess up, talk to Him, and get it right.

Chapter 10
How To Heal The Sick

The Healing Environment

By "healing environment" I am referring to the spiritual atmosphere surrounding a ministry encounter.

The ministry encounter could include healing the sick, casting out demons, or any other ministry requiring a demonstration of the Spirit's power.

When we approach such a ministry encounter it is essential that we give serious consideration to the healing environment.

Biblical Examples

Jesus is healing the sick in this passage of scripture. But the news about Him was spreading even farther, and large crowds were gathering to hear *Him* and to be healed of their sicknesses. Vs.17 One day He was teaching; and there were some Pharisees and teachers of the law sitting there, who had come from every village of Galilee and Judea and from Jerusalem; and the power of the Lord was present for Him to perform healing. (Luke 5:15,17 NASB)

Another example of Jesus setting the atmosphere. 39 And entering in, He *said to them, "Why make a commotion and weeping? The child has not died but is asleep." 40 And they began laughing at Him. But putting them all outside, He *took along the child's father and mother and His own companions, and *entered the room where the child was in bed. 41 And taking the child by the hand, He *said to her, "Talitha kum!" (which translated means, "Little girl, I say to you, get up!"). 42 And immediately the girl got up and began to walk, for she was twelve years old. And immediately they were completely astounded. (Mark 5:39-42 NASB)

Jesus said He could not do any miracle there except a few because of their unbelief. And He was amazed at their unbelief. And He was going around the villages teaching. (Mark 6:5-6 NASB)

Two Important Characteristics Mark A Healing Environment

Manifest Presence Of God - Expectant Faith

Personal Preparation For Ministry

- Ask for a fresh infilling of the Holy Spirit. Pray until you sense His anointing.

- Remind yourself of who Jesus is, what He has done, and what He must do.

- Do not forget, it is only through Jesus, and faith in Him, that the victory will come.

- Seek to empty yourself of "self." Remember that of yourself you can do nothing (John 15:5).

- Try to empty your mind of all preconceptions and presumptions concerning how the healing or deliverance will take place. It does not always have to be the same way.

- Ask God, "What do YOU want to do?" (SEE: John 5:19-20) Once you discover God's will in the matter, submit yourself absolutely to His will. You can now proceed in boldness and faith.

- Frequently pray in the Spirit, constantly listening for His voice to direct you.

How The Anointing For Ministry Comes

The gifts of the Spirit, including the three power gifts, come as "anointings" of the Holy Spirit: faith, healings and working of miracles.

Just how then do these anointings come upon an individual for ministry?

- Some testify of an inner surge or a sudden infusion of power, "heat," or "tingling"

- Others say that these anointings come with a feeling of deep compassion (Mark 1:41).

- A full assurance that the work will be done.

- A "knowing" that God wants the healing done

- A sudden confident faith that God will heal or work a miracle

- Do not put God in a box just yield and let Him flow through you

HOW TO HEAL THE SICK

Three important questions in the healing encounter:

1. What is the person's real need?
2. How will I proceed with ministry?
3. How will I advise this person after the ministry engagement?

Before I had some radical changes in my thinking and how I did ministry I used to have people come forward for prayer at the end of my sermon and I would walk along and pray for one and then go to the next and so on.

One day the Holy Spirit asked me, how do you know if they are healed? I said, well that is up to you Lord, and that is true. The Holy Spirit told me to start asking them, what is going on, check it out and see if they still hurt or if they still have the problem. So, I was obedient and started asking and to their surprise as much as mine, the pain was gone, they could bend or do something they could not do before.

That is when my whole ministry changed. The other revelation I had was how Jesus pulled away and prayed privately most of the time and then in public He ministered, He spoke and commanded sickness and pain to leave. He did not pray for the sick, He healed the sick. I personally pray privately over my day and my meetings. When I go out into public, I am healing the sick, setting the captives free, speaking, and commanding sickness, disease, and pain to go. I am speaking to bones to come together, hernias, tumors, and cancer to go in Jesus name. Nancy and I have been doing this for over 35 years and we are still amazed how God shows up.

Disclosure

Early in ministry Nancy and I understood that we were just yielded servants that God could flow through. Basically, we are nothing more than a hose for God. Along the way the Lord has showed us how to navigate and flow in the ministry of miracles, signs, and wonders. I am just showing you some of the things that have worked for us that others have used over the years.

I have ministered in miracles, signs, and wonders thousands of times; individually, church services, revival meetings and crusades around the world and each time it was a little different.

Sometimes I would get words of knowledge and I would speak them out, individuals would respond and get their healing, their miracle or breakthrough.

Other times I would give an altar call for healing and people would come forward and I felt faith rise in me. Then there were times I ministered and felt nothing, but I spoke out and ministered in the confidence of the works of Christ and His word and many were touched by the power of God.

The Interview

Step one in the healing encounter is to discover what the individual's real need is. We begin the healing encounter by asking a question:

"What would you like God to do for you today?" "How can I help you?"

Before proceeding with ministry, it is important to know what the need is and how you are going to minister to that person.

Ministry Engagement

The next step in the healing encounter is what I call the "ministry engagement." I now act based on my understanding of what they need and how I am going to minister.

I will ask the Holy Spirit to come and manifest His power.

I always invoke Jesus name in ministry.

I begin to minister healing through the laying on of hands, words of faith, commands of faith, declarations, petitions, teaching, the release of power, the prayer of agreement, binding and loosing or some other biblical method as the Holy Spirit leads.

As I proceed with ministry, I am constantly being sensitive to what God is doing.

I am watching for indications of the Spirit's work. People are feeling better, less pain, more movement in their body and limbs. There are times people are getting healed and there are no signs immediately, the next day they get out of bed totally healed, that happens often.

Do not stop too soon. Sometimes the healing is a process and takes time. Again, be led by the Holy Spirit.

If they have received healing, encourage them to continue in faith and obedience.

Jesus Ministry

A common healing method was Jesus spoke a word to the one being healed.

Another common healing method of Jesus was touching or laying hands on the sick person

Faith was and is a prime ingredient.

He was moved with compassion

Jesus did all His works in the power and anointing of the Holy Spirit.

Many of his miracles resulted from a release of power that flowed from Him into their bodies resulting in their healing.

Be a hose for God, be a conduit and allow Him to flow through you.

Conclusion: Today, we too, should seek to imitate the methods of Jesus with this one essential addition -- we must do it in the powerful Name of Jesus!

Chapter 11
Guard Your Mind and Mouth

Are Your Words Lining Up With God's Word

My wife Nancy preaches, teaches, and lives a message called, Guard your M & M's. Guard your mind and your mouth.

Guarding your M & M's is deep strategic spiritual warfare.

We are human, but we do not wage war as humans do. We use God's mighty weapons, not worldly weapons, to knock down the strongholds of human reasoning and to destroy false arguments. We destroy every proud obstacle that keeps people from knowing God. We capture their rebellious thoughts and teach them to obey Christ. (2 Corinthians 10: 4-5 NLT)

This shows us that we can do spiritual warfare with our minds (human reasoning) and our mouths (false arguments).

Guard Your Mind

There are many ways to do this, but I will just focus on two ways this can be accomplished. Please be aware that God's Word and the Holy Spirit have many ways to accomplish this so keep your eyes and hearts open if you want to walk in God's peace and joy.

Set your mind and keep it set

And set your minds and keep them set on what is above (the higher things), not on the things that are on this earth. (Colossians 3:2 AMP)

Paul clearly tells us to think about things that are important to God and doing them will fill our minds with good things.

To "set" your mind means to make up your mind firmly.

Wet concrete can be moved with ease and is very impressionable before it dries or "sets." But once it dries it is set in place for a long time and it takes a lot of work to move it.

This "concrete principle" also applies to your mind. To set your mind is to determine decisively what you will think, what you will believe, and what you will and will not do. Once you set your mind according to the truth of God's principles you need to keep it set and not allow outside forces or circumstances to reshape your thinking.

This does not mean to be narrow minded or stubborn. We should always be open to learning, growing, and changing for God's glory, but we must consistently resist the temptation of listening to the enemies lies.

We must make a choice every day to agree with God's word and His ways. The only way to agree with His word is to know his word. This comes by reading, studying, and hearing the word. We should not use the excuse, "I didn't know."

We Have The Provision, But We Must Partake

If we want to be debt free, we must set our mind on a budget and be determined to stick to it every day until we reach our goals. This works the same way with weight, with ministry, if we want change, we must have the right mindset and be willing to walk it out.

If we never set goals and set our mind to stick to them, we will not have the peace and joy God's wants us to have.

He said to them, "Why are you sleeping? Get up and pray that you do not come into temptation." (Luke 22:46 NASB)

For as he thinks within himself, so he is. He says to you, "Eat and drink!" But his heart is not with you. (Proverbs 23:7 NASB)

Our mindset determines how we will receive from the Lord. We must believe; He loves us, He desires to have us walk in healing, victory, and breakthrough.

Whatever we believe will show up in our decision and behavior.

And do not be conformed to this world, but be transformed by the renewing of your mind, so that you may prove what the will of God is, that which is good and acceptable and perfect.(Romans 12:2 NASB)

We are destroying arguments and all arrogance raised up against the knowledge of God, and we are taking every thought captive to the obedience of Christ. (2 Corinthians 10:5 NASB)

If we are told we are to take every thought captive into the obedience of Christ, then what He says, we can do.

We Think We Have No Control Over Our Thoughts, But we Do

Some of the wrong thoughts are criticism, prejudice, jealously and pride.

Renewing our minds is not a quick one-time event, it is an ongoing process that goes on until the day we die.

Wrong thinking will make us weak and keep us from God's best for us.

Let us study God's word, listen to the Holy Spirit and get a Kingdom mindset!

Guard Your Mouth

Death and life are in the power of the tongue. (Proverbs 18:21 NASB)

Wow! What we say is so important according to God's word.

Remember in Genesis we are told that God spoke this world into existence, His words are immensely powerful and because Genesis also says we are made in His image we know that our words are powerful too.

There are many ways to guard your mouth, let's look at a couple...

Say What God Says

Too often we want to state our opinion about things but all that really matters is what does God say about these things.

When we say what he says we will always be truthful, encouraging and uplifting with others and ourselves.

We can say " I am ugly" or "I can't do anything right" we are not telling the truth because God's Word says we are made in His image and that we can do all things through Him.

Why would we choose to say what the enemy says about us rather than what God says about us?

We also need to be careful about saying things like, "I think I am coming down with the flu." There are times we may talk about, my pain, my cancer, my condition, this stuff is affecting us, but we do not have to take ownership of it.

There are times I will be ministering healing to individuals with pain in their bodies and I will command the pain to leave in Jesus name and then ask them, do you feel any pain and they say, "not right now" and I will ask them are you expecting it to come back later.

I realize confession with our mouth is powerful and we need to be continually confessing God's Word, that does not mean we ignore the condition we are experiencing and be afraid to talk about it. Some people think if they talk about a condition, they are experiencing then they are accepting it as their lot.

We must be careful we do not over talk the conditions and problems we are facing. I have ministered to a lot of people over the years and many have been more into talking about their problems then getting a healing or a solution.

Speak With Authority

We need to speak in authority. I assure you and most solemnly say to you, whoever says to this mountain, 'Be lifted up and thrown into the sea!' and does not doubt in his heart [in God's unlimited power], but believes that what he says is going to take place, it will be done for him [in accordance with God's will. (Mark 11:23-24 AMP)

God's Word says in Isaiah, with the stripes that wounded Him we are healed and made whole. (Isaiah 53:5 AMP)

Disease, sickness, pain, negativity is not from God so we must investigate God's Word and see what He says about these situations, speak it out and take the steps of faith accordingly.

We need to be careful in saying, we don't have enough because God's Word says in Philippians, "And my God will liberally supply (fill to the full) your every need according to His riches in glory in Christ Jesus. (Philippians 4:19 AMP)

Our words need to line up with the Word of God. We must agree with God's Word rather than agreeing with the enemy.

Be Thankful

Enter His gates with a song of thanksgiving and His courts with praise. Be thankful to Him, bless and praise His name. (Psalm 100:4 AMP)

In every situation [no matter what the circumstances] be thankful and continually give thanks to God; for this is the will of God for you in Christ Jesus. Do not quench [subdue or be unresponsive to the working and guidance of the Holy Spirit. (1 Thessalonians 5: 18-19 AMP)

We need to be thankful to God and we need to be thankful to each other.

There is enough negativity in the world and from the enemy so we must choose to be thankful to God and others. A thankful attitude can change the atmosphere where we are from negative to positive.

In Texas when I say thank you to a waiter or waitress most of the time they reply, "It's my pleasure." That tells me their desire is to serve me and make my day better. That is what I call, a servant's attitude, we all need that.

Jesus said in Matthew, "just as the Son of Man did not come to be served, but to serve, and to give his life a ransom for many." (Matthew 20:28

NASB)

Jesus is our example, so we are to serve others and be thankful for everything.

How To Continue To Walk In Your Healing And Breakthrough

Throughout my years in ministry, I have witnessed numerous miracles that were breathtaking in nature: blind eyes and deaf ears opened, paralyzed walking, pain gone from herniated discs and radical deliverance from strongholds. Sadly, I have also witnessed some of these issues returned just days, weeks, or months after that healing encounter. And unfortunately, this happens all too often.

Why Does This Happen

I ministered to a lady a few years ago and she had been on oxygen for 12 years dealing with COPD. Even with the oxygen she could barely get around due to her difficulty with breathing.

One Sunday morning in a service I was ministering in, she came forward to receive a healing in her body. She told me her story that she had been a smoker and as a result was struggling with COPD.

As I was talking with her, I felt like the Lord was saying, I am going to give her new lungs. I told her what I sensed the Lord was wanting to do and she said she was ready.

I laid hands on her and spoke out what the Lord had revealed to me and declared the Lord was giving her new lungs.

After speaking that word, I said to her, what's going on and at that moment she took the oxygen hose out of her nose and began to walk around the sanctuary several times and then came back to me. As she stood in front of me without oxygen, she had no sign of being out of breath. She took off again and started running and then came back to me, not out of breath at all.

For the next two years she testified, spoke a woman's conferences about how the Lord had given her a miracle.

A little over two years later she had sent me a message that she had started smoking again and the breathing problems were back, and she was back on oxygen. What a sad story.

We must be so careful not to open the doors for the enemy to return.

The Process Of A Breakthrough Miracle

To understand how issues, return and how to prevent them from returning, we must first understand what takes place during a healing or breakthrough miracle.

In most every case, these miracles are a type of deliverance. The origin of sickness is not from God, it has a satanic origin and is dealt with accordingly.

It's understandable why the healings of Jesus are almost always activated by a rebuke or command, followed by the ailment leaving its victim, as in the case of Peter's mother-in-law: "So [Jesus] stood over her and rebuked the fever, and it left her" (Luke 4:39a NASB)

We also see this later modeled by the disciples in Acts. All throughout the book, the healings of Peter and Paul are each coupled with a command declaration.

I am not suggesting that every symptom, sickness or struggle you face is the result of a devil or personal sin. Some issues are simply the results of the weather, a fallen world, or a myriad of other possibilities. Thankfully, however, according to Jesus, it is not only unclean spirits that have to go, but He suggests that obstacles can too.

"Truly I say to you, whoever says to this mountain, 'Be taken up and thrown into the sea,' and does not doubt in his heart, but believes that what he says is going to happen, it will be granted to him." (NASB, Mark 11:23)

Here, Jesus used "mountain" as a metaphor for "obstacle," which, He assures, can be removed or "delivered." You can replace the word "mountain" for whatever it is that stands in your way—from a headache or a bad attitude to depression or physical pain.

In all this commanding and declaring for it to be effective we must be in alignment with God's word and His ways.

Why Issues Return

With this knowledge, you now understand that when someone receives a healing or breakthrough miracle, it is the result of some sort of deliverance that has taken place. And thus, we can learn from Scripture why these issues sometimes return and how to prevent that from happening to you.

Speaking about the process of deliverance, Jesus remarked, "Now when an unclean spirit goes out of a person, it passes through waterless places seeking rest, and does not find it. Then it says, 'I will return to my house from which I came'; and when it comes, it finds it unoccupied, swept, and put in order. Then it goes and brings along with it seven other spirits more wicked than itself, and they come in and live there; and the last condition of that person becomes worse than the first." (Matt. 12:43–45b NASB)

Jesus taught that what leaves is always looking for a way to return. If it is an unclean spirit, it will attempt to return with more. If it is some other sort of obstacle or stronghold, your mind or body will attempt to default to the way it used to behave unless you, teach it otherwise.

In either case, as Jesus instructed, the solution is to fill yourself with something to prevent its return. When we are set free of an unrighteous stronghold, we must immediately establish a righteous stronghold in its place.

How To Maintain Your Miracle

This brings me to back to guard your "M & M's" that maintain a miracle: the mind and the mouth.

The Mind

Many cite the high rate of return of symptoms from those healed at mass crusades. And the reason is clear: these events are not designed for follow-up discipleship. And so, a newly delivered individual often leaves without further instruction. The tendency then is to reenter life, not being cautious of the circumstances that once led to the afflictions.

Those with sustained victory are those who fill their minds with a constant diet of God's Word. This serves first to protect them from re-entering situations that might have led to the sickness or stronghold in the first place.

But second, it is to keep themselves standing on faith that what God did in the moment of their miracle is real. The enemy will try to reenter through temptation or doubt; and either one of those gateways, if not protected by God's Word, allows an opening for what left to return.

Filling your mind in this way is not difficult, but it is a discipline. If you were recently healed, find Scriptures related to healing. (Isaiah 53:5 KJV) is a great one to reflect upon: "But he was wounded for our transgressions, he was bruised for our iniquities; the chastisement of our peace was upon him, and by his stripes we are healed."

Similarly, if you were delivered of an addiction. (Romans 13:14 NASB) provides fantastic protection: "But put on the Lord Jesus Christ and make no provision for the flesh in regard to its lusts."

Whatever the situation, when the mind is fixed on truth, the enemy does not have even the slightest crack through which he can reenter.

The Mouth

Filling your mind with God's Word involves more than reading it; it also involves speaking it.

Scientists tell us our minds respond faster to what we hear ourselves say than what we "hear" ourselves think. This only confirms what Paul said so many years before: "So then faith comes by hearing, and hearing by the word of God." (Rom. 10:17KJV)

Faith is like an insect repellent to Satan or to any obstacle. And so, if you want to keep issues from having influence over you, the best way to fill yourself with faith is to make a habit of keeping God's Word on your mouth.

Stand on the Word of God

"Bless the Lord, O my soul, and forget not all His benefits: Who forgives all your iniquities, Who heals all your diseases." (Psalm 103:2-3 NKJV)

Do not let symptoms or circumstances talk to you.

"And being not weak in faith, he considered not his own body." (Romans 4:19 KJV)

Let Go Of Doubt

"And He did not do many miracles there because of their unbelief." (Matthew 13:58 NASB) So, if we are to receive from God, we need to position ourselves properly, have a right attitude.

My prayer is this word gets deep into you and you find yourself receiving and walking in the miraculous.

Chapter 12
We Need Signs and Wonders
Activating Your Faith

The "FULLY PREACHED" GOSPEL

The apostle Paul said to his generation: "I have fully preached the gospel of Christ." (Romans 15:19 NKJV) And he described the "fully preached" gospel as one that is much more than words. It is a gospel of words and deeds! "For I will not dare to speak of any of those things which Christ has not accomplished through me, in word and deed" (v. 18).

Paul was saying, "The Gentiles turned to Christ not because of my preaching alone, but because my words were accompanied by miraculous deeds!'"

"In mighty signs and wonders, by the power of the Spirit of God, so that from Jerusalem and round about to Illyricum I have fully preached the gospel" (v. 19).

If Paul had preached and taught without signs and wonders following, his message would not have had its full impact. It would not have been the gospel fully preached! He said to the Corinthians,

"Truly the signs of an apostle were accomplished among you with all perseverance, in signs and wonders and mighty deeds" (2 Corinthians 12:12 NKJV)

God is still God—and He is mighty in working miracles and wonders! He is still our healer and He wants to show Himself strong on behalf of those who trust in Him! Great supernatural workings took place in the New Testament church.

At Troas, while Paul was preaching a long message, a young man fell asleep while sitting on a windowsill and fell three stories to the ground. The Bible says the young man was "taken up dead"

In Acts 20:9-12 when Paul got to where the boy was, he quieted everyone. Then, just as Elijah had done, he stretched himself out over the dead boy and suddenly life came back into the young man. The boy had been resurrected—raised from the dead! What a mighty miracle!

After this happened, Paul did not send everyone out to spread the news that a miracle had taken place. No, that was not what happened at all. Everyone simply went back to the third floor, took communion, and Paul continued preaching. Scripture does not even mention the young man again. Why? Because the church expected supernatural works to happen! They preached a full gospel—with signs and wonders following!

More Than Preaching And Teaching

I believe the gospel should be accompanied by the power and demonstration of the Holy Ghost—working mighty wonders, proving the gospel is true!

Paul boldly stated, "And my speech and my preaching were not with persuasive words of human wisdom, but in demonstration of the Spirit and of power." (1 Corinthians 2:4 NKJV) The Greek here means "with proof."

Paul was saying, "I preach the gospel with proof. God and the Holy Spirit are backing me up with signs and wonders!"

Hebrews 2:4 says that God did confirm Paul's message with signs and wonders: "God also bearing witness both with signs and wonders, with various miracles, and gifts of the Holy Spirit, according to His own will."

The New Testament believers had one prayer: "That signs and wonders may be done through the name of Your holy Servant Jesus" (Acts 4:30). These apostles went everywhere fully preaching the gospel.

"Many wonders and signs were done through the apostles" (Acts 2:43). "And through the hands of the apostles many signs and wonders were done among the people. And believers were increasingly added to the Lord, multitudes of both men and women." (Acts 5: 12, 14 NKJV)

Signs & Wonders

Here is one of the most conclusive of all verses—proving that a fully preached gospel must include signs and wonders: "They stayed there a long time, speaking boldly in the Lord, who was bearing witness to the word of

His grace, granting signs and wonders to be done by their hands" (Acts 14:3). This verse says that the apostles ministered boldly for a long time, preaching grace and repentance, and then God granted signs and wonders to be done by their hands.

God's last-day church will go "out and [preach] everywhere, the Lord working with them and confirming the word through the accompanying signs" (Mark 16:20). That is what God envisions for us.

The miracles of this last-day church will be genuine, indisputable, undeniable, and yet they will not be well known. Instead, they will issue forth from the hands of ordinary, holy, separated saints who know God and are intimate with Jesus.

These believers will emerge from the secret closet of prayer—a small, prepared army full of faith, with no other desire than to do the will of God and glorify Him. They will be fearless and powerful in prayer. They will open entire nations for the gospel and God will confirm His Word by their mighty deeds!

Activating Our Faith

Revelation - Faith - Anointing – Manifestation

Gen 2:7 Then the Lord God formed man of the dust from the ground and breathed into his nostrils the breath of life; and man became a living being.

Revelation

We communicate with the Lord through our spirit not our soul. The Holy Spirit lives in our spirit and communes and speaks to us. This is where revelation comes from. I have a chapter showing how we operate between, spirit, soul and body that will bring you into a greater revelation.

When the Holy Spirit speaks the word comes from a perfect tense, it is complete, it is a done deal.

Faith

Faith is God inwardly persuading the believer of His preferences.

Anointing functions through faith, faith in what the Lord is saying and asking of you.

Faith is always a gift from God, and never something that can be produced by people.

God's divine persuasion – therefore distinct from human belief yet involving it.

The Lord continually births faith in the yielded believer so they can know what He prefers- the persuasion of His will. For whatever is born of God overcomes the world. And this is the victory that has overcome the world – our faith. (1 John 5:4 NKJV)

Faith is God's warranty that guarantees the fulfillment of the revelation He births within the receptive believe.

Faith involves hearing God's voice, through His word and through that still small voice.

Faith always comes from God and it always involves His revelation therefore faith is beyond belief.

Faith is always a response to a divine revelation!

Faith is an organ that enables people to see the invisible with our spiritual eyes.

It is the principle of faith operating in us.

Anointing

The anointing functions through faith.

The Spirit of the Lord God is upon me, Because the Lord has anointed me to bring good news to the humble; He has sent me to bind up the brokenhearted, To proclaim release to the captives And freedom to prisoners; To proclaim the favorable year of the Lord. (Isaiah 61:1 NASB)

The Holy Spirit Does Not Anoint, He Is The Anointing Himself

The anointing authorizes, gives you the authority and power to accomplish God's plan and purpose in and through your life.

When I get an intuitive thought from my spirit, a word of knowledge, by faith I act upon it and when I do, through that act of faith it releases the anointing, the authority and power to see that thing come to pass.

We call that a manifestation of God's glory, His tangible presence, a miracle, healing, or a breakthrough.

Anoint – means to set someone apart, to authorize and equip him or her for a task of spiritual importance.

Jesus Christ was set apart by the work of the Holy Spirit for His ministry of preaching, healing, and deliverance.

The Holy Spirit sets Christians apart for their ministry in Christ's name. Christos, the Anointed One. (2 Cor. 1:21-22 NIV)

Now it is God who makes both me and you stand firm in Christ. He anointed us, set His seal of ownership on us and put His Spirit in our hearts (spirit) as a deposit, guaranteeing what is to come.

When Jesus walked on this earth, His anointing was evident by the miracles he performed and the lives He touched.

As a follower of Christ, you have access to the same anointing.

Jesus said, truly, truly, I say to you, the one who believes in Me, the works that I do, he will do also; and greater works than these he will do; because I go to the Father. (John 14:12 NASB)

When you activate your faith, you follow in Abraham's footsteps as noted in Rom. 4: 17, 20-22

He believed in the God who brings the dead back to life and who creates new things out of nothing ... Abraham never wavered in believing God's promises.

In fact, his faith grew stronger, and in this he brought glory to God. He was fully convinced that God could do whatever He promises.

When you are staring death in the face – maybe physical death, the death of a dream, or the death of a relationship – it can be daunting to find the strength to activate your faith.

When all seems lost, this is precisely the time to activate your faith and believe that God will do exactly what he says He will do.

Your faith in Christ was not meant to sit unused on a shelf, but to be living and active, working in the trenches of your life.

Bottom line is your faith works when you work your faith.

How Do You Work Our Faith

You work out your faith by being in God's word, studying it, embracing it and living it out in our lives.

Two Blind Men

By expressing our faith, we must believe that, He is able. As Jesus went from there, (the official's house where the girl was raised from the dead) two blind men followed Him, crying out, "Have mercy on us, Son of David!" vs 28 And after He entered the house, the men who were blind came up to Him, and Jesus said to them, " Do you believe that I am able to do this?" They said to Him, yes, Lord. Vs 29 then He touched their eyes, saying, "It shall be done according to your faith." And their eyes were opened. (Matt 9:27-30a NASB)

Woman with The Issue Of Blood

Here we have a powerful example of this teaching and its application.

And a woman who had suffered a chronic flow of blood for twelve years, could not be healed by anyone, 44 came up behind Him and touched the fringe of His cloak, and immediately her bleeding stopped. 45 And Jesus said, "Who is the one who touched me?"

And while they were all denying it, Peter said, "Master, the people are crowding and pressing in on You." 46 But Jesus said, someone did touch Me, for I was aware that power had left Me.

47 Now when the woman saw that she had not escaped notice, she came trembling and fell down before Him, and admitted in the presence of all the people the reason why she had touched Him, and how she had been immediately healed. 48 And He said to her, "Daughter your faith has made you well; go in peace." (Luke 8:43-48 NASB)

This woman placed a demand on the anointing! She got a revelation if I could just touch the hem of His garment. She believed in her heart and went to where Jesus was, pressed through the crowd, by faith reached out touched the hem of His garment. Scripture says, immediately the anointing was released, the power and authority was released, and Jesus felt the anointing leave His body.

She was healed instantly. This is available for us.

Jesus is saying: From the days of John the Baptist until now the kingdom of heaven has been treated violently, and violent men take it by force. (Matt 11:12 NASB)

THE CENTURIAN

And when Jesus entered Capernaum, a centurion came to Him, begging Him, and saying, "Lord, my servant is lying paralyzed at home, terribly tormented." 7. Jesus said to him, "I will come and heal him." 8. But the centurion replied, "Lord, I am not worthy for You to come under my roof, but just say the word, and my servant will be healed. 9. For I also am a man under authority, with soldiers under me; and I say to this one, 'Go!' and he goes, and to another, 'Come!' and he comes, and to my slave, 'Do this!' and he does it." 10. Now when Jesus heard this, He was amazed and said to those who were following, "Truly I say to you, I have not found such great faith with anyone in Israel. 13. And Jesus said to the centurion, "Go; it shall be done for as you have believed." And the servant was healed at that very moment. (Matt 8:5-13 NASB)

When we are under authority, we can, just say the word.

The Glory

I want to speak to the manifest presence of God. The tangible presence of God.

The omnipresence of God, He is everywhere all at once. The omnipresence of God can exist without our awareness.

The manifest presence of God is His presence made clear.

We can have a perceived reality by what we are seeing and feeling, or we can have an objective reality grounded in the revealed Word of God or a Rhema word.

When Lord is speaking to me in my spirit, it is the Holy Spirit speaking to my spirit through the Word of God and/or that still small voice.

Now, I have received an intuitive word, a thus saith the Lord!

I received it in my spirit from the Holy Spirit which comes from a perfect tense (it is complete, it is a done deal).

Now with this revelation comes a divine persuasion, God is inwardly persuading me, faith wells up in me motivating me to action. I am know stepping out in faith, by speaking that word out, stepping through the door, taking some action.

My healing is not where I am sitting, my breakthrough, my miracle is not where I am standing, it is where I am about to step!

Faith Is An Action Word

Now that I have a revelation, put my faith in action it has released the anointing, the authority and power to see it manifested.

Now I am experiencing the manifest presence of God.

That is how it works!

Chapter 13
Operating From Your Spirit 1

Engaging The Kingdom

Jesus says, "The Kingdom of God does not come with observation; nor will they say, 'See here!' or 'See there!' For indeed, the Kingdom of God is within you" (Luke 17:20-21 NKJV)

Jesus is saying the Kingdom has already begun, speaking to the Pharisees it was right under their noses

God was already ruling in the hearts of some people, and the King Himself was standing among them telling story after story. (Matt 13:33 NASB)

If I drive out demons by the finger of God, then the Kingdom of God has come upon you. (Luke 11:20 NASB)

Kingdom is inward, it is within man's heart. The Kingdom is within your reach if you make the right choices.

Kingdom is in your midst in the person and presence of the Holy Spirit. This is where it all begins with mankind. Then the Lord God formed the man of dust from the ground (body) and breathed into his nostrils the breath of life (spirit); and the man became a living person (soul). (NASB, Gen 2:7)

Spirit, soul and body, the spirit is the part with which man communicates with the spiritual realm. The body is the part with which man communicates with the physical realm. The soul is in the middle of these two parts. It exercises its judgment to determine if the spiritual realm is to rule or if the physical realm is to rule.

Spirit

The spirit is the "God-consciousness."

Three parts: <u>Conscience</u> (spiritual conscience) I am telling the truth in Christ, I am not lying; my conscience testifies with me in the Holy Spirit, that I have great sorrow and unceasing grief in my heart (spirit). (Romans 9:1 NASB)

The Spirit Himself testifies with our spirit that we are children of God, and if children, heirs also, heirs of God and fellow heirs with Christ, if indeed we suffer with Him so that we may also be glorified with Him. (Romans 8:16,17 NASB)

The conscience is where we discern right from wrong, to justify or condemn.

<u>Fellowship</u> is for us to contact God and to commune with God. God is spirit, and those who worship Him must worship in spirit and truth. (John 4:24 NASB) For God whom I serve in my spirit in the preaching of the Gospel of His Son, is my witness as to how unceasingly I make mention of you. (Rom 1:9 NASB)

<u>Intuition</u> is a divine urge of our inner God. It means to have a direct sense or feeling in our spirit, regardless of reason or circumstance.

For who among people knows the thoughts of a person except the spirit of the person that is in him? So also the thoughts of God no one knows, except the Spirit of God. Now we have not received the spirit of the world, but the Spirit who is from God, so that we may know the things freely given to us by God. We also speak these things, not in words taught by human wisdom, but in those taught by the Spirit, combining spiritual thoughts with spiritual words. (1Cor. 2:11-13 NASB)

The spirit is the part with which man communicates with God. With this part man worships God, serves Him, and understands his relationship with God. Therefore, it is called "God-consciousness."

Just as God dwells in the spirit, self-dwells in the soul, and the senses dwell in the body. But in the beginning, man had not sinned, and the power of the soul was fully under the control of the spirit. Therefore, the power of the soul was the power of the spirit. The spirit could not drive the body by itself; it had to do so through the soul.

We can see this from Luke. And Mary said: "My soul exalts [present tense] the Lord, and my spirit has rejoiced [perfect tense] in God my Savior." (Luke 1:46-47 NASB)

Here we see the change in tense according to the original language, which indicates that the spirit must first exult before the soul can magnify the Lord.

The spirit first communicates the exultation, the exuberance, the feeling of triumph to the soul, and then the soul expresses this exultation, magnifies the Lord through the organs of the body.

The spirit is the part with which man communicates with the spiritual realm.

When the spirit controls the whole being, it is because the soul has yielded itself and has taken a lower position.

Paul speaks of the inner struggle. For what am I doing, I do not understand; for I am not practicing what I would like to do, but I am doing the very thing I hate. (Rom 7:15 NASB)

Dividing the soul from the spirit in Hebrews, clearly shows us that the spirit and the soul need to be divided and distinguished one from the other. It says, "For the word of God is living and active, and sharper than any two-edged sword, even penetrating as far as the division of the soul and spirit, of both joints and marrow, and able to judge the thoughts and intentions of the heart." (Hebrews 4:12 NASB)

If we are with the Lord, in an intimate place with Him and in His word, the Holy Spirit will divide our soul from our spirit by the word. He will show us through the word of God what is of our soul and not of the spirit, what we justify and what we condemn.

Through the word of God, the Holy Spirit always reveals to us the difference between the soul and spirit.

Soul

The soul is the "self-consciousness," Moral conscience can become seared. We can come to a place where we do not feel the pain of sin.

Example: I have ministered in leper colonies in India and I have seen where the leper has lost nerve sensation and when they hurt themselves many times, they are not aware.

It is like losing our first love, compliancy, indifference. Our moral conscience can receive inputs from our spirit, our flesh, or the world. That is where the dividing the soul and spirit comes in.

If we are not connected to God's word and intimacy with the Holy Spirit, we will become numb and not sense or feel the promptings, the love or even the convicting of the Lord.

The soul comprises that part of man known as the intellect, which makes man's existence possible. Love generates affections toward other human beings or objects. Affections originate from the senses. All these are parts of man himself; they form the personality of man.

Therefore, they are called the "self-consciousness." The soul is the meeting point, where the spirit and the body join. The soul lies in between these two worlds and belongs to these two worlds. On the one hand, it communicates with the spiritual realm through the spirit, and on the other hand, it communicates with the physical world through the body.

Processor

The soul has the power of self-determination; it can make decisions concerning the things related to it in its environment and can choose or reject them. It is impossible for the spirit to control the body directly; it requires a medium (processor). This medium is the soul, which was produced when the spirit touched the body. The soul is in between the spirit and the body; it binds the spirit and the body together as one. The spirit can rule over the body through the soul and subject it under God's power. The body can also induce the spirit through the soul to love the world.

The function of the soul is to maintain the spirit and the body in their proper order so that they will not lose their proper relationship with one another.

The soul looks to the spirit for the supply which the latter has received from the Holy Spirit and communicates to the body what it has received so that the body may partake of the perfection of the Holy Spirit and become a spiritual body.

The soul dwells between the spirit and the body and is the medium (the way of communication and intellect) of the two.

Unless the soul yields its rule to the spirit, the spirit cannot rule. Therefore, the soul must authorize the spirit to rule before the latter can rule over the soul and the whole body. The reason for this is that the soul is the origin of man's personality. The soul is the master of a person because man's will is part of the soul. Man's will (soul) has the power to choose to let the spirit rule, to let the body rule, or to let the self-rule.

Because the soul is so powerful, the Bible calls it "a living soul."

Body

The body is the "world-consciousness,"

There are five organs in the body which afford man the five senses. This physical body enables man to communicate with the physical world. Therefore, it is called the "world- consciousness."

Man communicates with the outside world of senses through the body; the world and the body interact with one another.

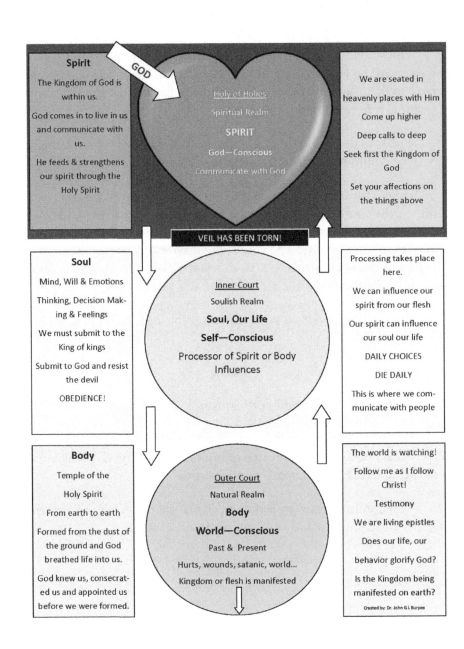

Spirit

The Kingdom of God is within us.

God comes in to live in us and communicate with us.

He feeds & strengthens our spirit through the Holy Spirit

Holy of Holies
Spiritual Realm
SPIRIT
God—Conscious
Communicate with God

We are seated in heavenly places with Him

Come up higher

Deep calls to deep

Seek first the Kingdom of God

Set your affections on the things above

GOD

VEIL HAS BEEN TORN!

Soul

Mind, Will & Emotions

Thinking, Decision Making & Feelings

We must submit to the King of kings

Submit to God and resist the devil

OBEDIENCE!

Inner Court
Soulish Realm
Soul, Our Life
Self—Conscious
Processor of Spirit or Body Influences

Processing takes place here.

We can influence our spirit from our flesh

Our spirit can influence our soul our life

DAILY CHOICES

DIE DAILY

This is where we communicate with people

Body

Temple of the

Holy Spirit

From earth to earth

Formed from the dust of the ground and God breathed life into us.

God knew us, consecrated us and appointed us before we were formed.

Outer Court
Natural Realm
Body
World—Conscious
Past & Present
Hurts, wounds, satanic, world...
Kingdom or flesh is manifested

The world is watching!

Follow me as I follow Christ!

Testimony

We are living epistles

Does our life, our behavior glorify God?

Is the Kingdom being manifested on earth?

Created by: Dr. John G L Burpee

Temple of God

Do you not know that you are a temple of God and that the Spirit of God dwells in you? (1Cor 3:16 NASB)

1Thes. 5:23 says, we are spirit, soul, and body.

After we clearly see God's order, we will see the wisdom God has in comparing man to the Temple of God.

We see how the Holy of Holies, the Holy Place and the outer court correspond with the order and the degree of importance of the spirit, soul, and body.

The work of the Temple revolves around the revelation in the Holy of Holies. All the actions in the Holy Place and the Outer Court are determined by the presence of God in the Holy of Holies.

In the Holy of Holies there is no work, it is a place of rest and communication and fellowship with God. The Holy of Holies is a quiet still place.

The Holy Place activities are directed by the inspiration of the Holy of Holies. Why is this so important to understand?

The Soul is the organ of our personality. It includes the mind, the will, and the emotions. The soul appears to be the master of the activities of the whole being.

Even the body is under its direction. Yet before man fell, although there were many activities and works with the soul, they were all under the control of the spirit.

God's order is spirit, soul, and body. The (spirit) is where we engage the Kingdom within us. The glory of God is in us! Our spirit is a place of perfect tense; it is a place of rest, his is where God communicates with us.

We must be intentional that the activities in the soul (Holy Place) expressed through the body (Outer Court) come from our communication and interaction from the spirit (Holy of Holies).

Receiving From The Kingdom

If you lead your life by your soul, you may feel anxious, uptight, or unsure of what you are doing. You worry about what people are thinking about you. You worry about the future; you dwell on the past. It is easy to get "stuck" in your soul. This is perfectly natural.

Most mental health issues are in the soul. That is where we primarily need healing to be spiritually, physically, and emotionally healthy. To move from living by your soul to being led by your spirit, there is a process.

First, you must become aware of your spirit through daily practice. We become aware of our spirit, we acknowledge our spirit's place, then we strengthen our spirit and let our spirit lead.

Become Aware Of Our Spirit

The first step is to become aware of our spirit and to begin to connect with it. Ask the Holy Spirit to teach you how to recognize your spirit. Close your eyes and take a few slow deep breaths. Imagine the Holy Spirit filling your spirit, filling you on the inside just like your breath fills you.

Asking for the Holy Spirit to breathe/flow in us is not that we are asking for more, we are asking for the winds /breath of /God to activate what is already in us.

Example: Billows on a cool source; wood or coal ambers. Damper on a fireplace closed causes a lot of smoke but when it's opened the air flows and the fire gets hot. We are told to stir up the gift 2 Tim 1:6, stir up the coals, recognize, be and do what God desires of us so we can truly walk in our God given purpose and destiny. It takes a lot of practice to become aware of your spirit. We are led by the Holy Spirit through our spirit.

Acknowledge Your Spirit's Place

As you begin to connect with your spirit, you will recognize what value it has. God created it for a specific purpose.

He will show you that purpose, to encourage you and strengthen

102

you.

We must believe that God wants to express and demonstrate His will and purpose through our spirit so that it will be manifested on this earth.

There is something special inside of you that deserves to be known to the outside world and that is God's will and purpose!

Each day ask God's Spirit to come and fill your spirit and wash it. Ask the Holy Spirit to lead you, guide you throughout the day. Ask for divine appointments. God's Spirit is the provider of all the resources you need to fulfill your destiny.

When you invite Him to come and fill you, breathe on you, He begins to direct your day and lead your steps (and you notice it). Holy Spirit and our spirit become one, we are born again in our spirit, brand new, heavenly influenced from the King of kings through the Holy Spirit.

Our spirit and soul are connected and when we are fully engaged with our spirit influencing our soul then we are truly declaring and demonstrating the Kingdom of God on this earth.

This is where we should be concerned, we must intentionally BE ENGAGED!

A motor vehicle is an awesome thing that has major abilities to function in many ways. There is this powerful motor with major horsepower that has great possibilities. There is this high-tech computer that does things that will blow our mind! We have a transmission that must be engaged to move forward.

If we do not engage the transmission, then we are missing out on a lot of; WHAT COULD BE!

Spend some time each day paying attention to your spirit and begin to acknowledge its value.

It is an education for your soul in who you really are.

Your soul may have heard many negative messages about who you are (i.e. you are stupid, you will never succeed, etc.). Think of all the negative things you have either heard or thought about yourself. It feels like your soul is drinking in those words.

John 10:10 read it. As you learn who you are in your spirit – God's DNA in you – you begin to see your own value, the value God put on you. You have a core value that no one can take away.

We know the devil comes to steal, kill, and destroy and we know God's desire is to give us life abundantly. It is so important to know who we are in Christ Jesus and how much He loves us and cares about us. It is important for you to look up each one of these scriptures and personally apply it to yourself.

Scripture Affirmation

First, ask God's Spirit to come and fill you and wash you of all that negativity and garbage, then I read these scriptures out loud to yourself.

Allow affirmation through God's word.

Who I am in Christ Jesus: I Am Accepted John 1:12 - I am God's child John 15:15 - I am Christ's friend Romans 5:1- I have been justified 1Cor. 6:17 - I am united with the Lord, and I am one spirit with Him. 1 Cor. 6:19-20 - I have been bought with a price, I belong to God.

Eph.1:1- I am a saint Eph. 1:5 - I have been adopted as God's child Eph. 2:18 - I have direct access to God through the Holy Spirit Col. 1:14 - I have been redeemed and forgiven of all my sins Col. 2:10 - I am complete in Christ I Am Secure Romans 8:1, 2 - I am free forever from condemnation Romans 8:28 - I am assured that all things work together for good Romans 8: 31-34 - I am free from any condemning charges against me Rom. 8:35-39 - I cannot be separated from the love of God 2 Cor. 1:21-22 - I have been established, anointed and sealed by God Col. 3:3 - I am hidden with Christ in God Phil. 1:6 - I am confident that the good work that God has begun in me will be perfected Phil 3:20- I am a citizen of God's Kingdom 2 Tim. 1:7 - I have not been given a spirit of fear but of power, love and a sound mind Heb. 4:16 - I can find grace and mercy to help me in time of need. 1 John 5:18 - I am born of God and the evil one cannot touch me.

I Am Significant Matt. 5:13, 14 - I am the salt and light of the earth John 15:1, 5 - I am a branch of the true vine, a channel of His life John

15:16 - I have been chosen and appointed to bear fruit Acts 1:8 -I am a personal witness of Christ 1 Cor. 3:16 - I am God's Temple 2 Cor. 5:17-21- I am a minister of reconciliation for God Eph 2:6 - I am seated with Christ in the heavenly realm Eph. 2:10 - I am God's workmanship Eph. 3:12 - I may approach God with freedom and confidence Phil. 4:13 - I can do all things through Christ who strengthens me.

I must CHANGE the conversation in my head and CHANGE the atmosphere in my head (the pervading tone or mood.)

My soul needs to acknowledge my spirit's place and my spirit is not going to feel confident to step out if it is constantly listening to the negativity coming from my soul.

Let Your Spirit Lead

The last step is to work with your spirit and your soul each day. Your soul is like a little child that needs protection from harmful influences. Your spirit was designed to do that. When your soul feels sad, lonely, fearful, rejected, etc., your spirit can give it what it needs in terms of encouragement, support, security, acceptance, etc. because of the presence of the Holy Spirit in your spirit.

Once you have become aware of your spirit and acknowledge that it has a right to be expressed, work on strengthening your spirit by embracing the truth then allow your spirit to lead.

Pray for the leading of the Holy Spirit everyday through your spirit!

It is time for activation!

Chapter 14
Operating From Your Spirit 2

The Demand Of The Kingdom Of God

Your kingdom come. Your will be done, On earth as it is in heaven. (Matt 6:10 NASB)

Everything that was lost in the Garden of Eden by Adam and Eve was restored by His death, burial, and resurrection our relationship with God, our health, our wealth, and much more.

Jesus is the reigning King, and His desire is to build His Kingdom through us.

A Kingdom mindset is an understanding of the Kingdom of God, the mind of Jesus Christ, the anointed One, the King.

Two things are particularly important to the King and His Kingdom.

Reign = His rule, reign, dominion, and authority.

Realm = community and territory.

How do we enter in to all that God has for us? Not only enter in, but obtain and walk in the blessings, power, authority, healings, and provision.

How do we enter that experience? For the Kingdom of God is not eating and drinking, but righteousness, peace, and joy in the Holy Spirit. (Rom 14:17 NASB)

How is the righteousness of the Kingdom of God obtained?

If we confess with your mouth Jesus is Lord and believe in your heart that God has raised him from the dead, you will be saved. (Rom 10:9 NASB)

The question is, is the Kingdom of God entered into by merely making a verbal confession that Jesus is Lord?

If we truly believe and confess, then we need to understand that when we do that the Kingdom of God makes one fundamental demand: The demand for a decision!

Jesus said, the time is fulfilled, and the kingdom of God is at hand; repent and believe in the gospel.; The Kingdom of God has come near. (Mark 1:15 NASB)

When Jesus said repent, He was talking about a change of heart (in our spirit) toward sin, the world and God: an inner change that gives rise to new ways of living that exalt Christ and give evidence of the truth of the gospel.

In the Greek repent: (Meta Noia) – Meta is a prefix that means, movement or change. NOIA – refers to the disposition of your inner self, your default setting "toward reality."

It means to have a transformed default setting about what is important to Jesus Christ, the King and His Kingdom. Jesus message was repent for the Kingdom of God is at hand!

The basic meaning of repentance is, to turn around, reverse the course of life, change direction and your actions, turn to embrace all that the King and His Kingdom has to offer.

Life is made up of decisions, the course of every person's life is determined by their decisions.

The difference between the successes of two people equally talented is determined by the way in which they make decisions. Some people go through life wavering back and forth, unsure of themselves, never able to say a distinct Yes or No.

The essence, substance, the principle of repentance is a decision which determines the quality of a present life and future destiny.

And as you go, preach, saying, 'The Kingdom of heaven is at hand has come near.' "Heal the sick, raise the dead, cleanse those with leprosy, cast out demons. Freely you received, freely give. (Matt 10:7,8 NASB)

The injunction, the legal order backed by the authority of Jesus that was given to His ambassadors was this: Heal the sick and say to them "The Kingdom of God is at hand". That is still how the Kingdom comes into our areas of influence! These preachers looked like ordinary people; they were declaring and demonstrating the Kingdom of God. The basis demand of the Kingdom of God is a response of our will. We must receive it. We must yield to it.

God's Kingdom does not ask us to find in ourselves the righteousness that it demands; God will give us the righteousness of His Kingdom. God's Kingdom does not ask us to create the life it requires; God's Kingdom will give us that life. God's Kingdom does not set up a standard and say, "When you achieve this standard of righteousness, you may enter the Kingdom."

God's Kingdom makes one demand: Repent! Turn! Decide!

Receive the Kingdom, as you receive its life, you receive its blessings, you receive the destiny that is reserved for those who embrace it.

Jesus requires from us a resolute decision, fixed with purpose, intentional.

"No one, after putting his hand to the plow and looking back is fit for the kingdom of God." (Luke 9:62 NASB)

If you respond to the Kingdom of God and its claims upon your life, there must be no hesitation, no looking back.

"As they were going along the road, someone said, to Him, "I will follow You wherever You go." And Jesus said to him, "The foxes have holes and the birds of the sky have nests, but the Son of Man has nowhere to lay His head." (Luke 9:57-58 NASB)

Serious Decision!

Jesus challenged the seriousness of his decision.

Do we really know what our decision involves?

Are we willing to become a disciple of one who is homeless?

Have we considered the implications?

Jesus demanded a resolute decision, an intelligent decision, one not made lightly.

In Luke, Jesus said to another, "Follow Me, But he said, "Lord permit me first to go and bury my father." (Luke 9:59 NASB) Here was a man who professed readiness to decide, but there was something else to be done first. "Yes, I want to follow but wait a while." "I have good intentions but give me a little time." Jesus answer seems harsh. "Let the dead bury their own dead, but you go and preach the Kingdom of God."

Now that is some serious stuff!

Urgent Decision

The Kingdom of God demands an immediate, urgent decision. I have heard others say, "I must live my life." "I have a career to pursue." "I have important plans for my future, and they are first." "I have other obligations."

But Jesus said these excuses won't work in the Kingdom of God.

We must respond immediately without delay! The next man in verses 61,62 says, "Lord I will follow You, but first let me go and bid them farewell that are at my house."

On the surface this seems a reasonable request but look at Jesus' response to him. "No one who puts his hand to the plow and looks back is fit for the Kingdom of God." Jesus is letting him and us know that there is no place for reluctance, no hesitation in the Kingdom of God.

Radical Decision

The Kingdom of God demands a radical decision! Some decisions are easily made and require little effort; but the decision for the Kingdom of God is often difficult and requires great energy and will. Jesus says, "From the days of John the Baptist until now the kingdom of heaven has been treated violently, and violent men take it by force. (Matt 11:12 NASB)

"The Law and Prophets were proclaimed until John came; since that time, the gospel of the kingdom of God has been preached, and everyone is forcing his way into it. (Luke 16:16 NASB)

The idea that Jesus was communicating was that before the time of John the Baptist, the only way to approach God was through the Old Testament laws and sacrifices.

In Jesus time these had become cold and empty rituals and the hearts of the people were far from God. When John the Baptist came in the power of the Spirit in Matt chapter 3 preaching a turning from sin to faith in the coming Messiah. They were truly (pressing in) to the Kingdom of God, overcoming any obstacle or opposition posed by the laws, traditions, unbelief or any satanic thing thrown at them, in order to receive the message John the Baptist preached.

They were violently resolved in their zeal and forcefully pressing into the Kingdom of God.

Today, as in the days of John the Baptist, Satan is opposing the preaching of the Gospel of the Kingdom, only those who are violently resolved, determined to receive God's best will receive it. Submit therefore to God. But resist the devil, and he will flee from you. (James 4:7 NASB)

We must force into, press in, place a demand on the anointing like the woman with the issue of blood.

The Kingdom of God demands a response so radical that it is described in terms of violence and force.

"If your foot causes you to sin, cut it off. It is better for you to enter life lame, rather than having two feet, to be cast into hell, into the fire that will never be quenched. (Mark 9:45 NKJV)

"And if your eye causes you to sin, pluck it out. It is better to enter the kingdom of God with one eye, rather than having two eyes, to be cast into hell fire. (Mark 9:47 NKJV)

"Do not think that I come to bring peace on earth. I did not come to bring peace but a sword. (Matt 10:34 NKJV)

110

A sword is an instrument of violence. Sometimes a decision for the Kingdom will be a sword the cuts across other relations bringing pain and suffering.

"Strive to enter through the narrow gate, for many, I say to you, will seek to enter and will not be able. (Luke 13:24 NKJV)

Strive – to strain every nerve. It is a common word used to describe physical conflict in athletic games.

All the language describes the radical character of the decision demanded by the Kingdom of God.

Too often we can find ourselves casual about serving God. Many can take radical measures in the pursuit of wealth, success, and power; but be unwilling to become deeply moved about the concern of our soul or even the souls of others.

We want the blessing and all that comes with the Kingdom, but where is our commitment?

We are running a race; we are at war! Jesus said, such a man cannot know the life of the Kingdom. It demands a response, a radical decision.

Costly Decision

The decision which God's Kingdom demands is a costly one.

A rich young ruler asks; "Teacher, what good deed must I do to get eternal life? (Matt 19:16 NIV)

The question shows there is a hunger for life in the Kingdom.

This man was showing a deep desire to find life, eternal life, in a realm beyond his earthly existence which is locked in by sin and death. With this young ruler the decision was not a simple or easy matter, it involved great cost.

Jesus looked into the young man's heart and saw what was holding him back from making this decision. The young man was rich, and Jesus saw that he was attached to his wealth. He knew that his wealth was standing in his way. Jesus told him, therefore go, and sell everything you have, and you will be free to follow Me.

God may not require us to forsake our wealth, but He does demand us to forsake our love for possessions. Where are our affections? We are to set our affections on the things above not on the things of this earth.

The Kingdom of God will cost us our life.

Jesus said, He who does not take up his cross and follow after me is not worthy of Me. (Matt 10:38 NKJV) Jesus ultimate price was the cross.

The cross represents dying to ourselves, and living in the resurrection power. The cross is always a reminder that it is a place of death.

To be absent from the body is to be present with the Lord. Think about that!

We think about that when we die physically, but think about when you die to the flesh, the things of this world. I find that the more I die to self and the things of this world the more I find myself sitting in heavenly places with Him.

Jesus said, Let him deny himself. Denial of self means death, nothing less.

In Burkina Faso, a minister and five others were killed by jihadists. They were told to leave their churches by these terrorists, and they chose to sleep in the church. This is what cross bearing means: readiness to die with and for Christ. It means a complete dedication to Christ. It is a life of total surrender, holding nothing back, not even life itself.

How Do We Do This

This takes place in our spirit and with a yielding of our soul it is fundamental in our relationship with Christ.

Cross-bearing involves the question of Lordship, Rulership, and Kingship. Christ cannot have rulership in your life until you count yourself dead and crucified with Him.

112

Eternal Decision

The Kingdom of God demands eternal decisions! The decision for or against the Kingdom of God determines a person's future destiny. There is a day of judgement. Christ one day will appear as the Son of man in glory and we all give an account. Will we hear, well done my good and faithful servant?

Christ has come among us to confront us with the blessings and demands of the Kingdom of God. Repent for the Kingdom of God has come near.

Receive it!

The Kingdom demands a decision, tomorrow has met today, and the age to come has entered this age. Thy Kingdom come; thy will be done.

What are we to do? One thing, REPENT, turn around, surrender to its rule in your life.

Jesus must be on the throne of our lives not our flesh. We must press in; this is a serious decision, a radical decision, a costly decision, and an eternal decision!

This is the demand of the Kingdom.

The Kingdom manifested on the earth is: Salvation, healing, miracles, deliverance, provision and empowerment.

When we submit to what the demand the Kingdom of God puts on us then we can place a demand on the Kingdom. We need to let Jesus look into our heart, allow the Holy Spirit to search us and show us what is holding us back, what do we need to repent of or surrender and just do it!

Releasing The Kingdom

Now we are positioned to place a demand on the Kingdom!

And a woman who had suffered a chronic flow of blood for twelve years, and could not be healed by anyone, came up behind Him (Jesus) and touched the fringe of His cloak, and immediately her bleeding stopped. And Jesus said, "Who is the one who touched me?" And while they were all denying it, Peter said, "Master, the people are crowding and pressing in on You." But Jesus said, "Someone did touch Me, for I was aware that power had left Me." Now when the woman saw that she had not escaped notice, she came trembling and fell down before Him, and admitted in the presence of all the people the reason why she had touched Him, and how she had been immediately healed. And He said to her, "Daughter, your faith has made you well; go in peace." "Daughter, your faith has made you well, go in peace." (Luke 8: 43-48 NASB)

Thy Kingdom come thy will be done on earth as it is in heaven.

When we submit to the authority of God's word and that, still small voice called the Holy Spirit, then we can place a demand on the Kingdom, the anointing and move in power and authority.

Kingdoms take territory and affect community How do we do that?

By getting into that spiritual realm hearing and seeing.

Declaring & Demonstrating the Kingdom!

We do it through: Salvations, healings, miracles, signs, wonders, deliverance, and empowerment.

We touch hearts, change minds, that changes behavior, changes culture, brings transformation.

Expectation Brings Manifestation

By faith we move in the anointing, the power of God that releases the glory of God.

The Glory of God, in His manifest presence there is: presence, there is power, there is peace, and there is provision!

Now faith is the substance of things hoped for, the evidence of things not seen. (Hebrews 11:1 NKJV)

114

Faith is an action word. We cannot be passive, indifferent, or casual about our mission, our destiny, our God-given purpose.

We Must Be Intentional

Our breakthrough, our miracle, our healing, our provision is not where we are sitting, not where we are standing it is where we are about to step!

Royal Priesthood

We are called to be kings & priests, not one or the other.

And has made us kings and priests to His God and Father, to Him be glory and dominion forever and ever Amen. (Rev. 1:6 NKJV)

"But you are a chosen people, a royal priesthood, a holy nation, a people for God's own possession, (1 Peter 2:9b NASB)

Righteousness is our relationship with the government.

Kingdom is our disposition, our placement in the government.

Kingdom is the horizontal dimension that deals with power: rulership. It is kingship!

Righteousness is the vertical dimension that deals with position, our relationship, right standing and authority. It is priesthood!

But seek ye first the Kingdom of God, and His righteousness and all these things shall be added unto you.

Kingdom is God's government; it is His rulership and dominion over heaven and earth. It means to have influence over territory, to impact and affect community.

If we are truly followers of King Jesus, our lives will reflect the influence of His government and administration in us and through us.

You will know them by their fruits. Grapes are not gathered from thorn bushes, nor figs from thistles, are they? So, every good tree bears good fruit, but the bad tree bears bad fruit, A good tree cannot bear bad fruit, nor can a bad tree bear good fruit. (Matt 7:16-18 NASB)

People will show how they are positioned, what kingdom they are a part of by what they produce in their lives.

If we want to be righteous, we must submit to Jesus Christ the King, for He is our righteousness.

It is only because of Jesus's death, burial and resurrection that we can stand rightly today.

By applying the word of God and living by His principles they keep us positioned properly so we continually have access to the King and all that He provides for our mission and purpose.

Righteous is right positioning, to be in alignment with the ruling standard, His word.

Demonstrating the Kingdom is; impacting community with God's will, His purpose and intent, producing a culture, values, morals, and a lifestyle that reflects the desire (de (of) sire (the father), the heart and nature of the King, Jesus Christ, the anointed One.

Divine Priority

First, Divine object – Kingdom of God!

Divine position – Righteousness!

We must first and foremost be positioned properly in God's Kingdom.

Alignment with His government is so important if we are to be effective in the Kingdom.

We must submit to the King's rule, reign, dominion and authority in our lives, our marriage, and our family.

Provision, power, protection, peace are by-products of our position in the Kingdom.

Holiness, humility, generosity, a servant's heart, and much more are by-products of our right standing our relationship with the King.

But seek first his kingdom and His righteousness, and all these things will be provided for you. (Matthew 6:33 NASB)

Alignment

Alignment with the word of God, the rule of His government.

Alignment with that still small Voice.

Alignment with our God given purpose.

When we submit, walk in obedience our access is unlimited, our direction is precise, our walk and influence is powerful!

By-products of Kingdom of God alignment: Fruit of the Spirit – not the fake plastic fruit.

But the fruit of the spirit is (result of His presence in us) love, joy, peace, patience, kindness, goodness, faithfulness, gentleness, self-control; against such things there is no law. (Gal 5:22-23 NASB)

We don't have to force it, it's not legalism. Vs 25 If we live in the Spirit, let us also walk in the Spirit.

Gifts of the Spirit - For to one is given the word of wisdom through the Spirit, and to another the word of knowledge according to the same Spirit; to another faith by the same Spirit, to another gifts of healing by the one Spirit, and to another the effecting of miracles and to another prophecy, and to another the distinguishing of spirits, to another various kinds of tongues, and to another the interpretation of tongues. (1 Cor. 12:8-10 NASB)

He will give us wisdom, knowledge and understanding, power and authority (spiritual) and they are by products of kingdom living.

Favor Again, it is about alignment with God's government, God's word. It is about alignment with our attitudes, our thinking, our relationships with the Lord, our spouse, our family, those in the workplace, those in our community.

We must be in agreement with God's word.

Esther came before the King and he extended his scepter, a symbol of authority, a symbol of righteousness, the king's favor. (Esther chapter 5)

When we are positioned properly, aligned properly, rightly standing in our government, the Kingdom of God, we have access to all the King has.

What is our purpose, our God given purpose?

God's favor is on our purpose, what is the Holy Spirit saying?

Do we have clarity of purpose?

Have we come into alignment with our purpose?

Are we intentional with our purpose?

Why is this so important?

Look at Joseph's life, God was with him, His favor was with him.

God's favor will bring collaboration, release finances and open doors of opportunity.

When you have heard from the King and He has given you a mandate and you chose to walk it out declaring and demonstrating you will see the Kingdom of God manifested on this earth.

The prayer of agreement, declaring and decreeing, that is how we engage, receive, place a demand, and release the Kingdom of God on earth.

Chapter 15
Conquering the Spirit of Fear

I know there are a lot of scriptures on fear and most of us can quote a few of them.

There are still millions of Christians that live in fear and worry.

The spirit of fear paralyzes us.

It stops us from stepping out in obedient faith and moving toward our destiny.

Today, I am going to take on the subject, of fear and I will cover it from a few different angles.

I will also show you some ways to deal with fear.

Fear has a wonderful, protective benefit for us when it functions as God designed it.

Fear, terror, alarm, and worry threaten to derail our faith.

We are called to take captive every thought, and trust God.

Fear Is A Lack Of Trust In God And His Word

The Lord is our protector, defender, provider, and healer.

When I am afraid, I put my trust in You. (Psalm 56:3 NASB) No matter what we may be going through, we can put our trust in the Lord.

"Do not fear, for I am with you; do not be afraid, for I am your God. I will strengthen you and help you; I will uphold you in My righteous hand." (Isaiah 41:10 NASB) but by God's word and through prayer from His perspective **we can choose to trust** that if He says not to fear, we don't need to be afraid.

A healthy fear of God fuels our faith.

We can respond to fear by redirecting what is scaring us to aligning it with God's word.

What does God's word say about this?

What is the Holy Spirit saying about this?

Fear's Evil Scheme

Fear is a tool the devil uses against us to make us miserable and destroy our lives. It begins as a thought and then creates emotions that can rule us.

It often becomes a strong, intense feeling that tries to move us to make foolish decisions or tries to prevent us from doing something that would be good for us.

Because it's such a common way that satan attacks people's lives, I think of it as the demonic spirit he uses to manipulate people and keep them out of God's will.

Simply put, fear is the opposite of faith.

God wants us to walk by faith, and satan wants us to walk by fear.

When we learn to live by faith and not let fear rule our life, we can live a fulfilling, satisfying, peaceful and joyful life in Christ. Like I said before, fear begins with a thought.

(Proverbs 23:7 NKJV) tells us that "as [a man] thinks in his heart, so is he." I like to say it like this: Where the mind goes, the man follows.

Living In Fear Reveals A Lack Of Trust In The Lord

I have a hard time trusting a stranger, I do not know them well enough to believe and act upon what they are saying. The greater my relationship with that stranger the greater my trust.

Fellowship Vs Communion

I really feel like the Holy Spirit brought this to my attention and it is something we need to take a hard look at!

A lot of Christians today seem to use them interchangeably, and they both seem to be quite popular in our mission statements, vision statements and slogans.

Fellowship

Fellowship is more of a basic concept. It refers to the relationship between a group of people who have something in common, like community, religion, or friendship.

Fellowship in the church is about Christians spending time together. Christians spending time together, bowling, going to the movies even Bible studies or small groups.

Fellowship is important in the life of the church though; it is not an end goal.

This is where the problem lies. Much of the church considers going to the house of God, worshipping and meeting with one another is their purpose and life as a Christian. That is an important part of our life and we should not forsake the assembling of ourselves together, as the manner of some but exhorting one another; and so much more, as ye see the day approaching. (Hebrews 10:25)

Communion

Communion is more complex, much deeper than fellowship, communion is about being in union together (com-union).

Fellowship: Time and activity spent together doing similar things.

Life shared alongside one another.

Communion: Time and activity spent together doing the same things.

Life is shared and exchanged with one another.

A good example of communion is marriage. The union of husband and wife as two becoming one flesh. Their lives are not just similar or parallel, they are shared and exchanged.

God invites us to become one with Him, to share communion with Him.

But he who is joined to the Lord becomes one spirit with Him. (1Cor 6:17 NKJV)

One With Christ

What shall we say then? Are we to continue in sin so that grace may increase? Far from it! How shall we who died to sin still live in it? Or do you not know that all of us who have been baptized into Christ Jesus have been baptized into His death? Therefore, we have been buried with Him through baptism into death, so that, just as Christ was raised from the dead through the glory of the Father, so we too may walk in newness of life. For if we have become united with *Him* in the likeness of His death, certainly we shall also be *in the likeness* of His resurrection, knowing this, that our old self was crucified with *Him*, in order that our body of sin might be done away with, so that we would no longer be slaves to sin; for the one who has died is freed from sin.

Now if we have died with Christ, we believe that we shall also live with Him, knowing that Christ, having been raised from the dead, is never to die again; death no longer is master over Him. For the death that He died, He died to sin once for all *time*; but the life that He lives, He lives to God. (Romans 6:1-1 NASB)

After an individual is justified by faith in Christ, he discovers that he still has a sin nature. This gives him trouble, and he finds himself committing sins that he does not wish to commit. Soon he may become a believer who is dominated by sin.

Solution

The solution to this problem is our identification with Jesus Christ in His death and resurrection. In this identification God sanctifies, or makes holy, the justified individual (saved by grace).

Whereas justification deals with the guilt of sin, sanctification

Identification deals with the power of sin in the life of the believer.

How does God sanctify, or make holy, a believer in daily experience? Romans 6 gives the answer. The answer is our union, or identification, with Christ.

Notice again that everything we have is because of Christ. Being in union with, or identified with, Christ is what is meant throughout the New Testament by the expression "in Christ." Being in Christ simply means that the believer has become one with Christ or identified with Him.

Christ is not just a partner walking alongside the believer; He indwells the believer. Therefore, the believer is identified with Christ because Christ's life is in the believer.

"I have been crucified with Christ; and it is no longer I who live, but Christ lives in me; and the life which I now live in the flesh I live by faith in the Son of God, who loved me and gave Himself up for me. (Gal 2:20 NASB)

So Let Me Get Back To Trust And Fear

How do we build our trust in the Lord?

How do we grow in faith?

The greater our communion with the Lord, the deeper our relationship, the deeper our relationship, the deeper our trust and with that, we grow in faith.

We know the Father, we know His heart, we know how He sees us, what He thinks about us. We know about His protection, His provision, and His healing power.

We know God's desire for us. For I know the plans that I have for you, 'declares the Lord, 'plans for prosperity and not for disaster, to give you a future and a hope. (Jer. 29:11 NASB)

We know His voice!

God has a purpose for us, a destiny and it is through this communion we establish clarity of purpose, we establish trust, and we grow in faith.

Keys To Conquering Fear

1. Realize that God is with you.

Do not fear, for I am with you; Do not be afraid, for I am your God. I will strengthen you; I will also help you; I will also uphold you with My righteous right hand.' (Isaiah 41:10 NASB)

The Lord is for me; I will not fear; What can man do to me? (Psalms 118:6 NASB)

Even though I walk through the valley of the shadow of death, I fear no evil, for You are with me; and Your rod and Your staff, they comfort me. (Psalm 23:4 NASB)

2. Trust in God - I heard it said, "Every opportunity to fear is also an opportunity to trust God.

3. Seek the peace of God

4. Be filled with God's love - Perfect love casts out all fear.

5. Fear God - The fear of the Lord is a fountain of life, by which one may avoid the snares of death. (Proverbs 14:27 NASB)

6. Be strong and of good courage- Have I not commanded you? Be strong and courageous! Do not be terrified nor dismayed, for the Lord your God is with you wherever you go." (Joshua 1:9 NASB)

7.   Pray - Have communion, establish an intimacy with the Holy Spirit, communicate with Him, daily communion.

We Don't Have To Live In Fear

We can walk in confidence and boldness. We can trust and move in great faith but it is going to take more than just having fellowship it is going to take communion, intimacy, knowing the Father's heart, hearing His voice and trusting in and moving in Faith seeing the hand of God move in you and through you.

I can pray and command fear to go and it must go.

I pray the Holy Spirit reveals the importance of this revelation and shows you how to move into being one with Christ, in Christ, in communion with Him so you will walk in your true identity, knowing the power and authority you have over the evil one, knowing the power and authority you have over sickness, know the power and authority you have over fear, knowing the power you have in rebuking the devourer keeping him from sucking the life out of you and the resources you have.

Chapter 16
Taking Territory

The Walls Are Coming down

In Joshua chapter 6 we see an incredible event play out right in front of us. It was a strategy for victory. Joshua got a word from God, he believed it and the people with him believed, they acted in faith, did it exactly God's way and they got the victory.

Now the walls have crumbled, what are they going to do? They are going to take the land. We have all been given land and territory to conquer.

Now it came about after the death of Moses the servant of the Lord, that the Lord spoke to Joshua the son of Nun, Moses' servant, saying, "Moses My servant is dead; so now arise, cross this Jordan, you and all this people, to the land which I am giving to them, to the sons of Israel. Every place on which the sole of your footsteps, I have given it to you, just as I spoke to Moses. From the wilderness and this Lebanon, even as far as the great river, the river Euphrates, all the land of the Hittites, and as far as the Great Sea toward the setting of the sun will be your territory. No one will *be able to* oppose you all the days of your life. Just as I have been with Moses, I will be with you; I will not desert you nor abandon you. Be strong and courageous, for you shall give this people possession of the land which I swore to their fathers to give them. (Joshua 1:1-6 NASB)

Territory

Merriam-Webster - A geographic area belonging to or under the jurisdiction of a governmental authority.

Dictionary.Com – A field or sphere of action, thought

Territory: some form of structure and power relation, it has a form of government. That power relation is of the kingdom of darkness or Kingdom of light.

When I talk about territory I am not talking about rivals, about being territorial with a person, church, or ministry that tries to be more successful than another.

In ministry there should no rivals, rivals cause division, rivalry is about competition.

When we apprehend the territory that God has assigned us, we are not trying to compete with the enemy or trying to be better than the enemy.

All God's Territory Is Superior And Second To None

Territory is unlike space. The of space/ spatiality is understood as property or condition of that space or something pertaining to it.

Territory has a more active connotation. We are not speaking of the status of the territory, but the mode of operation within that territory. What is the function in that territory?

Territory is the basis of power. We are talking about the power of the Kingdom of God. Kingdom of God territory reflects the heart and ways of the King of kings and Lord of lords.

Territories require constant focus, intentionality to establish strategies, to affect, influence and change the hearts of man.

Territory has history, mindsets, culture such as drugs, alcohol, prostitution, pornography, human trafficking, corruption, political and business.

You have made them into a kingdom and priests to our God, and they will reign on this earth. (Rev 5:10 NASB)

Our role as kings is to rule over our own spirits, to overcome the world and the evil one.

Our role as priests is having access to the King of kings, a personal relationship, and access to all He has provided to accomplish our God given assignment.

But you are a chosen people, a royal priesthood, a holy nation, a people for God's own possession, so that you may proclaim the excellencies of Him who has called you out of darkness into His marvelous light. (1 Peter 2:9 NASB)

We are called to take and apprehend territory, change mindsets and culture.

We must displace power and principalities by bringing the light of Jesus Christ, the King of kings who is always advancing His Kingdom, the Kingdom of God

As a royal priesthood we are to conquer, acquire, administer, and adjudicate within that territory so that it engages what the devil has possession of that belongs to God's people.

We are called to administrate Kingdom authority over the earth but do it with a priestly heart.

We are called to the nations!

We are called to be lovers of God and warrior kings who take possession of enemy territory for Kingdom rule.

We must have a Kingdom mindset!

Jesus wants to apprehend, establish, and occupy territory in our own lives. He wants to have rule, reign, dominion, and authority in our mind, will and emotions.

He wants to affect, and influence how we think, make decisions and how we feel about things and people.

We are in a battle and there is always revelation in the battle, a higher purpose than the fight itself.

On the battlefield there is a fresh revelation of who you are becoming, an identity for you to step into.

There is always increase and upgrade on the battlefield.

David knew that and that is why he ran towards Goliath. It was the attitude that made him a man after God's own heart.

The current difficulties you face will define for you a new place of identity.

The enemy will reveal to you the hand of God upon you.

God Always Wins

For us to overcome, we must face the battle the same way God does. We fight from victory not towards it.

We are warriors and a warrior mindset is always focused on victory.

The object to warfare is victory; the object to victory is occupation.

We take and hold territory in our identity in Christ Jesus.

You are the hope of the nations.

Go desires to bring heaven to earth through you.

Through your God given assignment you do this.

It is time to rise, apprehend, establish, and occupy all that God has set before you.

God wants to reveal how He sees you, His plan and purpose for you.

God's purpose, His favor is more on His purpose than on you as an individual.

Your promises have territory attached to them.

For the enemy to defeat you he must defeat you from inheriting, taking the land.

Do not fight the enemy on his grounds or by his ways, Fight from a higher ground.

Removing a poverty Spirit, poverty spirit keeps you trapped in a lower form of being

Poverty

Poverty is not about economic deficiency, true poverty is the acceptance of meager possibility

Poverty is accepting a limitation and being governed by lack. We convince ourselves we lack resources, but the reality is we do not go out to meet the provision. We are not stepping out in faith; we are waiting for it to come to us.

The Lord places provision not where you stand but where you are about to tread. It is in front of you, one step ahead of a poverty mindset.

Never let yourself be governed by externals, bank balance, your resources, your environment. Be defined by My permission then such as you have, I will always multiply.

We are Kings Kids; it is time to take the land!

We must take the land, apprehend, occupy and influence, being the salt and light, bringing transformation. God gets the glory.

Are we ready!

Will we just take up space or are we committed to take territory?

Thy Kingdom come thy will be done on earth as it is in heaven.

Kingdoms take territory and affect community

How do we do that?

Declaring and demonstrating the Kingdom!

We do it through: Salvations, healings, miracles, signs, wonders, deliverance, and empowerment.

God touches hearts, changes minds, changes behavior, changes culture and brings transformation.

Expectation Brings Manifestation

The Glory of God, in His manifest presence there is power, there is peace, and there is provision!

Now faith is the certainty of things hoped for, a proof of things not seen. (Hebrews 11:1 NASB)

Faith is an action word.

We cannot be passive, indifferent, or casual about our mission, our destiny, our God-given purpose. We must be intentional!!

We are called to be kings & priests, not one or the other.

And He has made us into a kingdom, priests to His god and Father to Him be the glory and dominion forever and ever. Amen. (Rev. 1:6 NASB)

"But you are a chosen people, a royal priesthood, a holy nation, a people for God's own possession, so that you may proclaim the excellencies of Him who has called you out of darkness in His marvelous light; (1 Peter 2:9 NASB)

Righteousness is our relationship with the government.

Kingdom is our disposition, our placement in the government.

Kingdom is the horizontal dimension that deals with power and rulership. It is kingship!

Righteousness is the vertical dimension that deals with position, our relationship, right standing and authority. It is priesthood!

But seek ye first the Kingdom of God, and His righteousness and all these things shall be added unto you.

When I talk about Kingdom I am talking about God's government, it is His rulership and dominion over heaven and earth. It means as citizens of the Kingdom we should have influence over territory by impacting and affecting community.

If we are truly followers of King Jesus, our lives will reflect the influence of His government and administration in us and through us.

You will know them by their fruits. Grapes are not gathered from thorn bushes, nor figs from thistles, are they? So, every good tree bears good fruit, but the bad tree bears bad fruit. A good tree cannot bear bad fruit, nor can a bad tree bear good fruit. (Matt 7:16-18 NASB)

People can tell how you are positioned, what kingdom you are a part of by what you produce in your life.

If we want to be righteous, we must submit to Jesus Christ the King, for He is our righteousness. It is only because of Jesus's death, burial, and resurrection that we can stand rightly today.

By applying the word of God, His principles keep us positioned properly so we continually have access to the King and all that He provides for our mission and purpose.

Righteous is right positioning, being in alignment with the ruling standard, His word.

The first part of demonstrating the Kingdom is; impacting community with God's will, His purpose and intent, producing a culture, values, morals, and a lifestyle that reflects the desire de, (of) sire, (the father), the heart and nature of the King, Jesus Christ, the anointed One.

Divine priority – First

Divine object – Kingdom of God

Divine position – Righteousness

Order and alignment with His government is so important if we are to be effective in the Kingdom.

We must submit to the King's rule, reign, dominion and authority in our lives, our marriage, and our family.

Provision, power, protection, peace is a by-product of our position in the Kingdom.

Holiness, humility, generosity, a servant's heart, and much more are by-products of our right standing before the King.

Alignment with the word of God

Alignment with that still small Voice.

Alignment with our God given purpose.

When we submit and walk in obedience, it makes our access unlimited, our direction precise, our walk and influence powerful!

By-Products Of Kingdom Of God Alignment

Fruit of the Spirit – not the fake plastic fruit

But the fruit of the spirit is (result of His presence in us) love, joy, peace, patience, kindness, goodness, faithfulness, gentleness, self-control; against such things there is no law. (Gal 5:22-23 NASB)

Gifts of the Spirit

For to one is given the word of wisdom through the Spirit, to another the word of knowledge according to the same Spirit; to another faith by the same Spirit, and to another gifts of healing by the one Spirit and to another the effecting of miracles, and to another prophecy, and to another the distinguishing of spirits, to another various kinds of tongues, and to another interpretation of tongues. (1 Cor 12:8-10 NASB)

Alignment brings, wisdom, knowledge and understanding

Power & Authority (spiritual)

Favor

Again, it is about alignment with God's government, God's word.

Our attitude, our thinking, our relationship with the Lord, our spouse, our family, those in the workplace, those in our community must be in alignment.

We must agree with God's word.

Esther came before the King and he extended his scepter, a symbol of authority, a symbol of righteousness, and the king's favor.

When we are positioned properly, aligned properly, in right standing in our government, the Kingdom of God we have access to all the King has.

What is Your purpose, your God given purpose?

God's favor is on your purpose.

What is the Holy Spirit saying?

Do you have clarity of purpose?

Have you come into alignment with your purpose?

Are you intentional with your purpose?

Why is this so important?

Look at Joseph's life, God was with him, His favor was with him.

God's favor will bring collaboration, release finances and open doors of opportunity.

When you have heard from the King and He has given you a mandate and you chose to walk it out declaring and demonstrating you will see the Kingdom of God manifested on this earth.

I want to encourage you to apply the principles in this book, get clarity of your God given purpose, be intentional and you will have an awesome journey.

Conclusion

Being Intentional With My Life

If you have not committed your life to Jesus Christ or are not sure about your relationship with Him pray this prayer and mean it in your heart.

Lord Jesus, I thank You for dying on the cross for me, shedding Your blood for the cleansing of my sins. I believe You died on the cross, was buried, and rose on the third day. I believe as I ask You to come into my life, that same Spirit that raised You from the dead now, dwells in me.

Lord, I personally ask You to forgive me of all my sins, cleanse me of all unrighteousness. I ask You to come into my life as Savior of my soul and Lord of my life. I make this commitment in Jesus's name.

Please email me if you have made that commitment so I can pray for you.

john@johnburpee.com

May God's blessings and favor follow you.

About The Author

Dr. John G L Burpee is the husband of Nancy, a beautiful wife and best friend. Together they have two adult children and five grandchildren. He served in the U.S. Air Force for nine years, serving three of those years in Southeast Asia. John pastored for 25 years in Maine, Missouri and Nebraska and now oversees Destiny Churches & Ministries International that he founded in 2005. He has traveled to 36 nations ministering in healing crusades, leadership conferences, Bible School and Church plants.

Dr. John G. L. Burpee exists to serve others by empowering expectation to experience the supernatural and achieve destiny. His heart to see people walk in their potential and live lives filled with purpose compels him to equip and activate. He is a bridge builder—connecting people and resources together so others can develop, grow, and step into their full measure.

A visionary and a strategist, John assists leaders in articulating their dream, developing their vision, and creating strategic systems that advance teams in the direction of stated goals. As a master networker, he is an invaluable resource to emerging leaders, helping them gain access to key relationships and proven tools for leadership development. With confident authority, he activates people to receive their portion and walk securely in their calling.

John Burpee moves comfortably in the supernatural. Without flash or hype, he confidently connects to God's power—power that is available to every believer—and moves in miracles, signs, and wonders. He travels extensively and the fruit of his ministry is evident in testimonies of salvation, healing, and being filled with the Holy Spirit. John not only declares God's Word, he demonstrates it. He is a true believer in the manifest presence of God.

Education:

- John has an extensive education in Aircraft Electronics.
- Certified Life Coach – Keith Johnson Ministries
- Diploma – Ministerial, Missionary 3 years at Faith Bible College – Charleston, Maine
- B.A. – Bible – Central Bible College – Springfield, Missouri
- Classes at Assemblies of God Theological Seminary
- M.A. – Christian Education – Destiny College International – Spring Hill, Florida
- D.Min – Destiny College International – Spring Hill, Florida

Ministries:

John Burpee Ministries – www.johnburpee.com

Destiny Churches & Ministries International – www.bridgetodestiny.com

DBA – Bridge To Destiny Ministries

john@johnburpee.com

Made in the USA
Monee, IL
06 June 2021